The Psychic's Wife;

Lifting The Veil

Published by
Ghostwriter Publications

ISBN 978-0-9957753-6-7

For my friend;

Your tear – my heart.

Books about psychics, though well-received, are ever destined to dwell in the bijou realms of the niche genre. The Mind-Body-Spirit section of your local book store is sure to carry a few, and you might be forgiven for anticipating some degree of similarity between them. But have you ever stopped to think about what life is like, not for the mediums, but for those who share their lives? What do you imagine your life would be like if your spouse was in regular contact with dead people, and knew just a little more about your day than you are comfortable with? How would you cope with a house full of ghosts? Could you get by without having your little secrets? It is a little-documented perspective, making this fly-on-the-wall insight a real third-eye opener.

David Drew is one of those mediums whose books you may have perused. As the wife of this internationally renowned psychic and author, I have spent many a long hour making cappuccinos for, chatting to, and answering questions posed by a selection of apprehensive and excited callers, all eager to spend time with my exhausted, caffeine-fueled other-half. This regular cacophony of spiritually orientated enquiries led me to realise that living with a psychic, while unremarkable to me, is the source of some fascination to 'normal' people.

After years of being told I should write a book, I have at last embraced the challenge and agreed to lift the veil on this mysterious lifestyle. I have endeavored to address such common questions as, "Does he read *your* future?" and "Can he tell what you are thinking?" as well as "Does he see dead people *all the time*?", "Aren't you scared?" and even, "If spirits are all around us, are they watching me when I'm on the toilet?"

The sitter's preferred question, 'Is he any good?' always draws a weary smile. It puts me in mind of that other famous inquiry to which there is no appropriate response, 'Hands up if you have stopped beating your wife!' When I reply, (in all sincerity), that he is the best and most uniquely gifted medium in the world, I am greeted with a smirking, "Ah, but you would say that," leaving me to puzzle over what response they were expecting. I am often tempted to tell them he is crap, just to watch their reaction, but I doubt people would appreciate, or indeed deserve the sarcasm. I confess, my reply is often preceded by an inadvertent eye roll, which is probably more than a little unfair.

The information within these pages is gathered from my up-close-and-personal vantage point. I am not the all-seeing eye. I have elucidated answers to the more technical spiritual questions from my darling, who stands on the bridge between two worlds.

I am a regular person, just like you, but I have had the unique opportunity to observe and learn from one who knows; who sees beyond normal sight and who remembers his time in the spirit-world before he was born.

So here it is, a first-hand overview of life with a psychic medium, as viewed by his wife, who is happy to be almost as invisible as the spirits which surround him. You may have heard the saying, 'love me; love my dog.' With David, it was always more of a, 'love me, love my spooks' situation.

Princess Diana once famously said, "There were three of us in this marriage".
I can tell you now without a flicker of fancy, there are a darn sight more than three in ours!

The Day That Changed My Life

Settle down, get comfy, and let's have a gossip. Make a coffee, plump the cushions, break open the biscuits and we will recreate the ante-room where, over the years, I have shared my secrets with those waiting strangers who were to be my bosom friends – for an hour or so at least.

I have chosen to start with the most frequently asked question. Yes, we did meet as a result of David's work, and no, he didn't see it coming!

I should perhaps lay some groundwork, and explain that mediums, generally speaking, are unable to heal themselves or predict their own future. This is reasonable when you consider it, otherwise they would have an unfair advantage over others, thus negating their raison d'etre. (Psychic gifts being bestowed for the benefit of other people, and not intended to be used for selfish purposes.)

David's spirit helpers saw the runaway train that was to be our relationship, hurtling towards him, but they dutifully kept their council. He was as surprised as I when we met and fell in love, in what might be considered a 'whirlwind' romance. With hindsight, I am certain we were fated to meet, no doubt the result of some greater force at work, but for now, I will stick with the earthly logistics of our love affair.

Ours is a story of soulmates, love at first sight and happy-ever-after. For more than thirty years we have been devoted to each other - which is not to say we have not had some spectacular rows. My personal favourite ended in a brussel-sprout fight so momentous it is still talked about today. (Okay - so only by us and the children, but still!)

I was born to stand in the wings. I had no childhood dreams of being the leading lady; the prima ballerina. Even my name is inconspicuous. Just Jane. Plain Jane. I like it that way, never having nurtured any desire to be noticed. But although I was never a leader, neither was I prepared to blindly follow. This set me apart socially, fated to remain slightly out of step with the crowd.

School was a bear pit. Not that I was either liked or disliked. The truth is I went largely unnoticed. Children can be cruel and shallow. From my social periphery, I observed girls rising and falling from their popularity pedestals, based on which band they liked or how they wore their hair. This wasn't for me, so I lowered my head and quietly watched these absurd gladiatorial games from my emotional hiding place. I had a couple of good pals who were neighbours, but at school, I kept largely to myself, except for a few casual friends who were similarly displaced. We would seek each other out at playtime, like a group of young elk avoiding the gaze of the circling, ravenous lions.

Home was my safe-haven.

I especially loved the garden; the red-hot pokers and bulbous-bottomed spiders, who walked shimmering tightropes over silver safety nets. Boys on the street would collect toads from the beck, dropping them onto the flagstones like kamikaze aircraft. I would run behind them, stealing the stunned animals and releasing them into the long, damp grass. I couldn't fathom this lack of respect for living things. Even today, if I have to kill a fly, I give a little scream. It doesn't happen often. I hate doing it. The family call me 'the reluctant swatter.'

Life was tranquil in the lazy, rural town of Retford, North Nottinghamshire, (much as it is in Llandudno, North Wales, where David and I would eventually settle). Both are great towns to grow up in or retire to, so long as you do something more exciting in-between.

Mum and Dad doted on me; their youngest child and only girl. Mum lived for her kids, and for years went without so that we would want for nothing. On the foundation of unconditional love, one can build a mansion. I could have built a palace were it not for the character flaws I managed to create all by myself, as the years did their damage.

My brothers, Alan and Paul, were older; so much so that I felt like an only child. As the girl Mum and Dad thought they would never have, I was spoiled – with love as well as material things. Despite this, I never quite felt I belonged to this world.

It was as though life was a sinister dream, and I couldn't quite remember what it was to be awake. The hint of a sense I had left some other, brighter place behind, rattled around the catacombs of my spirit like a penny dropped into a bottomless well.

My father was raised in a modest stone cottage next to the village watermill. He adored his mother who, long before I was thought of, went to sleep with a headache and never woke up. Her absence left a void in Brook Cottage (and in my father, I suspect) that would never be filled.

Dad worked his way up from the factory floor to become manager of an engineering company. He regarded himself as working class, although he was erudite and gentlemanly. A country boy and son of a collier, he was the first of his family to graduate from grammar school.

As was the mode of the day, Dad was proud that his wife didn't need to go to work. My mother was a devoted stay-at-home wife and mum, until the day she left him almost thirty years later. At sixteen, I was spared the fallout of an acrimonious divorce, as their combined sweet natures dictated they remain good pals until the day he died in 1998, but Dad always said I missed out on the 'daft lass' stage of growing up, going from child to adult in a flash. Perhaps the breakup was the reason. I tried to remain neutral but always worried that my dad would think I sided with Mum, as I moved to Blackpool with her.

The decision was actually more to do with geography than ethics.

It was after they split that I began to seek out my place in the adult world. There is nothing like seeing the unshakeable crumble, to make you realise you must find your own raft to cling to. I had dropped out of my A levels to move away, and now, at seventeen I entered the world of work. I took my ten O levels to the Job Centre and resolved to take the first position that would have me. This turned out to be fitting and selling children's shoes. Now I could pay my way.

I was able to move out of the flat I was sharing with my mum, and rent a place of my own to share with my Siamese cat. Today, when the settee is in the same room as the cooker, they call it 'open-plan'. Back then it was a bedsit. It was big enough for a bed and my keyboards, (music being my muse of choice), and that was all I needed.

I learned how to be independent and to rise or fall by my own decisions - which I did quite dramatically over the next year or two. I was young and made some foolish choices, notably in the relationship department, culminating in the realization that ultimately, when it came to men, I much preferred the cat.

They say there is a right time for everything. It was well into the 1980s before David and I met.

It was those magical years of the Sony Walkman, big

hair, Wham, and Maggie Thatcher. For about two weeks, I had been back, staying with my mother in Blackpool.

At the time I was reeling from a breakup. The short, toxic relationship, had left me homeless and, ironically enough, determined never to look twice at another man.

Mum had heard that Psychic Medium, David Drew – a 'proper' spiritual medium - none of your tarot-reading malarkey – was going to be appearing in the town. In an attempt to lift my spirits (no pun intended), she purchased tickets a month before to the event. The welfare of her brood ever the priority, she sensed that I was unhappy and had been largely motivated by the opportunity to remove me from my domestic environment, for a mother/daughter weekend, so I could 'get things off my chest.' What should have been a two-day break, however, had evolved into my temporarily moving in with her, after the flare-up of a sudden and particularly nasty argument finally brought things to a head and I walked out into the night air with a holdall and hardly a backward glance.

When Mum first told me she had seen a poster for some spiritual medium, I was mildly intrigued. Oddly enough, I had recently been given a couple of Doris Stokes books, and our family were no strangers to the supernatural, so the possibility that the dead could communicate was not an alien concept.

I feel inclined to mention at this point, that if measured with the normality yardstick, I come from a moderately weird family. I was raised on various, casually recounted stories of premonitions and first-hand encounters with ghosts. They predominantly stemmed from my mother's side of the gene pool; in particular the female members of the tribe. I am sure that most families have their ghost stories, usually tucked away in the closet like Great Aunt Mabel's commode, and only wheeled out in the appropriate circumstance.

My point is, I had been weaned on enough of these anecdotes to nurture, if not a fascination for, at least a cautious appreciation of the fact that we live on after death, and that two-way communication is a distinct possibility.

My family also believed in God and saw no paradox in this. My father had been an altar boy and we sporadically attended the parish church of Saint Michael when I was a child. At five, I played Doubting Thomas in their Easter Passion Play. It was a brave if uninspiring performance. I had one line, which was delivered from behind a strategically draped tea-towel, positioned to disguise the fact I had a dental abscess that had overnight turned me into a giant hamster.

Between the ages of eleven and fifteen, I was a member of my local church choir. (I could only just carry a tune, but enthusiasm compensated for my lack of any vocal skill.)

It was here I met and was ditched by, my first boyfriend, who left me in favour of a slightly older and bustier chorister, who was deemed, quite rightly as it turned out, more likely to 'put-out'.

But I digress.

The point I am trying to make is that, with hindsight, my pre-David life nurtured a vaguely spiritually orientated mindset, which proved the perfect prelude to my post-David life, as the wife of an attractive, loving (and flawed) man, who spoke to the dead, and even more bizarrely, supported West Bromwich Albion Football Club!

So, my mum's decision to buy tickets for a psychic event, though unexpected, was not entirely out of character. She had experienced many paranormal events herself, including predicting her apparently healthy father's sudden death, locating my paternal granddad's missing insurance papers (after being directed by a spirit voice), as well as having a two-way conversation with her deceased mother-in-law, while travelling to said lady's funeral.

Although in life they had their differences, my grandmother was comforting my mum with such comments as, "Never mind Lass, you got a new outfit out of it!"

My mum smiled in response, which raised a few eyebrows from other mourners in the limo, especially when a truck cut between the funeral procession, and my deceased grandmother laughed loudly in her ear, shouting to the driver, "Ayup! It will be your turn next!"

We never know the minute, but the wonderful truth is, neither do we know, when we open our eyes in the morning, if this could be a remarkable day we will remember all our lives.

On the morning of the psychic event, I woke to the smell of bacon and the sunlight streaming onto my face from the bedroom window. As I stretched out like a swastika, it took a moment to remember where I was, and I closed my eyes again to help drag my thoughts into some kind of order. To be honest, all I wanted at that moment was a duvet day. I was in Mum's double bed, comfy and warm; a little girl again. Everything was alright, if uncertain. I had my life back. My world had rebooted and my future was a blank slate for me to doodle on as I pleased. I had no idea where I was going, but at last, I was free to go there.

I nursed my indecision all day, and by early evening I had gathered enough motivation to make a half-hearted effort at making myself presentable.

The streets were all but deserted by the time I headed out with my mum into the English summer rain. The empty pavements were strange for a Saturday evening, but then it was still early, and the violent bursts of wind were unpleasant and unseasonal, even for blustery Blackpool.

The moment we stepped outside, my hair began to lash wildly around my face, and I quickly lamented not having better secured it. Mum had hurried me out of the door, and as we walked, I pictured with regret the wooden paddle hairbrush resting atop my red suitcase in her hallway. I had intended to drop it into my handbag as we left. By the time we reached the venue, I was confident I would look like Kate Bush fresh from her wild and windy moor.

Mum's steps were two to my one as we strode on with the suppressed desperation of the British, aiming to reach our destination and procure a favourable seat. I caught a few handfuls of the dark-brown, matted cotton-wool, which had been so sleek and shiny when I set off, and stuffed it into my raincoat, causing the top button to ping and bounce through the puddles on the promenade with all the exuberance of Barnes Wallis' finest.

"Leave it!"
I shouted into the wind at my mother, who, ever the economist, had stopped dead and was weighing up the odds of successfully retrieving it.
Then, softening my tone, aware that I had perhaps spoken sharply.
"Come on. We don't want to be late."

At that, her heels were clip-clopping beside me once again.

By the time we arrived, the theatre was humming with people eager to claim their seats.

I merged with them as Mum made her way toward the bar to order my requested coke and a coffee for herself.

The décor was opulent, with rich, Victorian reds, gold moldings, and an elegant antique Italian clock, which indicated we had arrived just in time.

The room was beginning to hush as I selected two seats - close enough to see the stage, but far enough away to be inconspicuous. Perfect. As the lights were lowered, I wondered if this guy would be genuine, confident that I could sniff out a fake. Although I believed that there was something in all this, I was no-one's fool. We could always leave at the interval if we were unimpressed.

When David nervously took the stage, I was surprised at how ordinary he looked; more like an estate agent than a psychic medium. I was expecting some flamboyant character, oozing bags of confidence and perhaps a little arrogance. This guy looked almost reluctant to be standing up there; the centre of attention, with all eyes on him.

The applause was starting to subside by the time Mum settled beside me, desperate to whisper something. I shushed her. The smartly dressed, slightly built young man was clearing his throat to talk. The room fell silent.

I remember how he began.

"This body you see before you, for what it's worth, will one day be burned or buried, but the soul; the spirit; the *real* you, lives on. Forever."

As he spoke, a curious sensation swept over me. It was surreal. I drifted past his metal-framed glasses, into those cornflower blue eyes, and somehow felt that I knew this man. It was impossible, but I fancied I even understood what he *wasn't* saying; what he was feeling. I glanced around at the crowd. Did they feel it too?

The audience were hanging on his words, as he explained how he needed to talk for a few minutes, allowing time for those in the spirit world, which is all around us, to begin to speak to him. He told of a childhood world of dead aunties pushing him on swings and spirit children playing hide-and-seek. He spoke of predicting the arrival of long-lost relatives and how the still-born sister he knew nothing of, introduced herself to him one bedtime when he was just a boy.

Soon messages from the spirit world began to flow and he forgot his nerves, becoming outwardly confident; pre-occupied yet strangely focused.

Despite this, there was an undercurrent of vulnerability. I sensed an invisible weight on his shoulders; perhaps a burden he was carrying alone? Just my imagination? Maybe! My mind was certainly drifting. I concluded that I must be losing my grip on reality, and dragged myself back to focus on the real world, dismissing any rambling thoughts.

I watched as David moved across the stage, noticed him begin to relax. He stood about five feet eight inches tall. His moustache and short hair were the colour of autumn. I smiled at his endearing, nervous habits, rolled my eyes once or twice at his humour as he risked a joke or two. I didn't know his favourite colour, where he was from or what he liked to eat, but somehow, I knew *him,* the way you are comfortable with a close friend you have known all your life.

I am sure you can guess where this is going, but I want to emphasise that I was most definitely *not* looking for romance that day. I had taken a step back from the world, needing time and space to re-assess my life. My plans did not include another relationship, but somewhere, silent pinions were turning and my plans were of little consequence.

If there was a type I usually go for, I would say it is tall, clean-shaven with dark hair and eyes. This guy was nothing like that, yet there was an attraction I couldn't ignore. There was a breath of heaven about him. Emotionally I felt a pull; a connection. Practically, I was disillusioned with relationships and had constructed a protective barrier to distance myself from any prospective suitors.

The evening was an intriguing experience, without question, but at that moment, I did not envisage it to be any more than that. I certainly didn't anticipate that I would ever encounter Mr. David Alan Drew again.

When the messages from spirit stopped and he announced a twenty-minute break, people were audibly disappointed. The lights went up and Mum couldn't wait to speak.

"That a man who stood next to me at the bar, said he's a bit psychic. When he looked across before, he said he could see a coal miner and American Indian Chief standing behind you."

She looked excited. I raised an eyebrow. True to say my granddad had been a collier, but Pocahontas I ain't! I scolded her for encouraging him and suggested this stranger was probably a little too drawn to spirits of the bottled variety. We chatted in our seats as people milled around us.

"Why don't you make an appointment to see this David Drew? He seems like a genuine lad. You've had it rough lately. He might be able to help."

It was true, I must have seemed somewhat lost. While I was happy to have shaken free from my emotional shackles, I had no idea what my next step should be, and she knew it. That said, I had no intention of making a nuisance of myself by pestering this lovely man, or indeed anyone else, for advice.

I dismissed her suggestion. I could sort myself out. I just needed time.

I decided to avail myself of the facilities, before the second half began, and left my seat in search of the ladies' room. People were filtering toward me, resuming their positions. I knew the interval was ending soon, and I would have to hurry, not relishing the prospect of making myself conspicuous by pushing past people in the dark to reclaim my seat.

I swiftly located the rest-room, then, mission accomplished, hurried back to the lobby, which was now deserted, except for one other person; a slim man in a dark, tailored suit - David Drew.

I caught my breath. Mum's words came back to me as I quickly considered the opportunity now presenting itself. Was fate giving me a push?

David was standing in front of me, and without thinking further, I took a chance.

"Hi. I really enjoyed your talk. I don't suppose you can see anything with me?" I could tell I was putting him on the spot and instantly regretted my intrusion.

The question seemed to hang in the air, as we stood face to face for the first time. There was a vastness behind this man's eyes. Like looking into a galaxy. They gave a momentary flash, then he quickly swapped his inquisitive gaze for a smile.

"Um, I can't do anything right now - but call me."
He fumbled through his jacket pockets and finally produced a pen.

Shifting awkwardly, he searched for something to write on, finally selecting a screwed-up receipt. "Call me," he repeated, meeting my gaze with a warm smile, then he dashed into the auditorium just as he was being introduced back onto the stage.

As the applause waned, I took my seat in the dark and quietly unfolded the paper.
'Twenty Benson & Hedges Gold £4.95….' and a phone number.

"You nearly missed him!" Mum whispered as I settled next to her. "He's starting."

David continued to pass on messages to the enthralled audience and I stared on; first at the paper and then at those eyes, wondering if I should call him.

Around a week later I picked up the phone on an impulse. A man's voice answered. David was out, but the man had his diary, and a home visit was arranged for the following week.

The designated evening soon arrived. As I put the kettle on there came the tap at the door, and swinging it open, the sight took caught me off-guard. There stood David on the door-step, formally dressed in a crisp white shirt and striped tie. My heart flipped in my chest! Composing myself I made the tea. His demeanor was friendly and polite; very professional.

We sat on the couch, making small-talk for ten minutes

or so, as we relaxed into each other's company. He was new to the area; staying with his friend, Tom, who was acting as his receptionist until he got settled. It seems he needed someone to help him get organized. Then the conversation lulled and the messages began to flow.

"Just give me a minute or two. I need to 'tune in', just like an old radio. Don't be afraid to talk back to me. A lot of people think they have to sit in silence. If there is anything I say that you don't understand or you want to ask any questions, feel free.

There may, of course, be one or two people in the spirit world wanting to say something. There usually is. Don't worry if it takes you a moment or two to place them. It is not always who you expect, and it may be going back a little bit.

First of all, I am looking at the aura around you. All my life I have seen people with an aura. As I tune in, I can see there is a lot of confusion surrounding you at the moment. Like a grey cloak all over you. Although I appreciate that you can't see it, I would be very surprised if you can't feel it. It isn't bad news. It's just because of the confusion around you."

He paused as if in thought. "Before I go any further, I want to work on that confusion and hopefully advise you on the future, from spirit. I always say to people, 'I am not a fortune teller.' A lot of people who see me want their fortune told, and I don't do that.

With the help of my spirit guide, we advise as to the way you are going and hopefully help you with any problems there may be."

He told me I was facing some crucial decisions; that I was at a crossroads in my life. "Behind you, I see a separation, a parting of the ways, but the door is still open if you want to go back." I knew this was true, but I most definitely was not going back. He told me about a new potential relationship ahead. I was doubtful of this. There was no-one in the wings and I had not the slightest desire to jump back into that particular fire. I explained that I was unaware of this possibility. He paused as though listening to someone, then asked if I knew someone called David. I didn't. "Oh. Perhaps they were just talking to me. Maybe someone trying to get my attention" He mused.

"I always say that life is like a book. When we've finished one chapter we have to go on to another. Although we can flip back the pages and take a walk down memory lane, we should always be looking forward and not backward."

"Regarding where you live, it's all change. I wouldn't be surprised if you weren't moving very soon. I don't know whether you've planned this or not, but there is definitely a move for you before the year is out. Spirit are encouraging this. You will be much happier after you move. By the end of September, you will at least know where you are going with your life."
Next, he described my grandma in great detail.

"I've got a lady here. Elderly before she went to spirit. Only small, about five feet tall. She has grey hair and, I hope she doesn't mind me saying, a big backside. She wears an apron and walks with a severe limp. The dining chair in her house, where she always sat, was facing the window; next to the fireplace, with a table to her left."

My mother's mum died when I was fifteen, but he painted a picture which brought her back like it was yesterday. "With her is a man calling 'Bill'. I presume that's William but he says, 'don't say William 'cos she won't know'. He stands at the back of you with a man he calls Jack." Uncle Bill and Uncle Jack were my grandmother's brothers.

The messages were fast-flowing once they began. This one giving some detail of proof, that one a gem of advice. His eyes drifted as he spoke, focusing over my shoulder or above my head, silently acknowledging some invisible countenance. He wasn't quite present as he listened to voices from other worlds, sometimes pausing to seek clarification from them, or apologizing that he had missed some remark.

When at last it was time to go, I was surprised to observe that David looked washed out. I felt suddenly guilty that this had taken so much out of him, and sincerely thanked him for his help as we walked to the door.
(In the years that followed, I would become very familiar with this drained look. I grew protective of

his strength. Each time David used his gifts, a piece of him was lost. His batteries could be recharged, but a toll was taken. There was a balance to be struck between helping people and diminishing himself.)

At the threshold he paused. "I passed a pub on the corner of the next street. What's it like?"
I told him I had never been inside, and he asked if I would like to join him for a drink, adding that being new to the area and had not yet made many friends. I accepted, without agenda. Perhaps, we were both lost souls in that moment.

It was only a short walk to the pub and the night was pleasant. As we entered the lounge bar, he caught hold of my hand with a warm but strong grip.

I was a little shocked, but it felt curiously right; like coming home on a dark night. My heart glowed in my chest, but I tried to keep my head. This was surely not the time to jump into a relationship.

"I hope you don't mind." He apologised as we found a table, "I just wanted to walk you past that group of men by the door."
The last of the gentlemen, I thought.

We were last to leave the pub that night, lingering over our drinks, and when he walked me home the place was deserted, but he took hold of my hand again. I met his gaze and raised an eyebrow.
He blushed and shrugged an explanation.
"I liked it on the way in."

The next morning, Mum and I had made preparations for a fun-filled day at the launderette. Dirty washing packed up and ready to go, I opened the front door, to find a startled David poised on the step, bearing a jeweller's gift box and an embarrassed expression. I had been unsure if he would ever contact me again, and most certainly did not expect to see him so soon.

The jewellery was a gift; a star-themed necklace and some earrings. It was a sweet gesture. I took very little persuading to ditch the laundry, and instead we took a stroll to nearby Stanley Park.

We walked the ornamental gardens, fed the ducks, lingered on the iron-work bridge that spans the lake, then wandered across the well-coiffed lawns, before stopping to take rest on a bench. We stayed there all afternoon. The sun was high in the sky, synonymous with the mood of the day.

Love is spectacular and brutal. It makes you vulnerable. To trust another being with your love and your life, and believe they will not destroy you, is a huge gamble. We step onto the tightrope and hope we don't fall, but if we never take that step, then we never really know what it is to live.

Despite my reservations about love, I liked this man. I liked his humour; his body; his touch. More than that, I loved his fearless wisdom, his fathomless heart.

I squeezed the hand that had held mine all day.
"Take off your glasses."

"Why?" He shifted uncomfortably.
"I just want to see your eyes."

Hesitantly, he removed his tinted specs. I had never seen eyes so blue. These were impassioned, resolute, tender eyes that I knew I could easily worship. They promised to ruin all my plans.

He replaced the silver frames and nervously examined my face for the verdict.
I gently kissed his lips in reply.

As the sun began its scheduled descent, we parted on the memory of a perfect afternoon, and the anticipation that what we had found might just be something spectacular.

The next day he came to see me again. It was unexpected and I was out, shopping in town with my mum. Even though I had no warning of his visit, he still chides me for this snub. He apparently spent the afternoon pacing the park, searching for me and nursing his disappointment. I have never understood the logic behind this. Perhaps he thought I aimlessly wandered around the flower beds every day.

A daily meeting was soon part of our routine, despite which, we wrote each other long letters, pouring out our feelings or rejoicing in our fortunes at finding each other. I particularly enjoyed his romantic, corny, but heartfelt poems, which I treasure to this day.

In an endearing attempt to impress, he pretended he

didn't smoke much and only took one sugar in his tea (which he consumes in copious amounts!)

There are intimate things you don't need to know. The smell of his hair, his strong, safe arms. For such a motivated man, he was strangely shy and blushed when I called him Darling. He said that when God made man, He split him in half and that each person doesn't feel complete until they find their other half. He told me how he thought he had loved before, but now he had found his other half.

It was a whole week before he proposed, telling me that when he first saw me he knew I was the girl he wanted to marry. Of course, I made him wait. I secretly had little doubt that we might-well spend our lives together, but it would be reckless to rush into marriage so quickly, and to be honest, it pleased me a little to keep him in suspense.

"We can wait if you want," he would shrug, "but what's the point? I will marry you one day, why not now?"

In the end, of course, true to the theme that would be our lives, he was right. We were married exactly one year from the day we met, in an intimate service one sunny, August morning. The day was perfect!

Years later, when our daughter, Ayesha, was five, she asked me when the happiest day of my life was. I answered truthfully, without raising my eyes from the ironing board. "The day I married Daddy."

She smiled up at me sweetly, then after a short pause added, "No Mummy, what was it really?"

Even though we have lived most of our matrimonial life in North Wales, we often re-visit Stanley Park on our anniversary. In those early days we vowed that if things didn't work out, we would go back on that day in August, to where we first walked and fell in love, and perhaps find each other again, in what will always be our special place.

Our home has always been filled with laughter, despite the inevitable troubles that life brings. It is the secret to a happy marriage. When we were young we laughed a lot, and now we are older we laugh even more – usually when we get undressed. Laughter is a serious business.

Practical jokes and good humoured banter has always been part of our dynamic.

I remember one year when Valentine's Day fell on a Sunday. In those days David habitually spent Sunday afternoons in the pub. It was a predominantly male habitat, and I knew it would be awash with testosterone and bravado. I couldn't resist.

Next door to his local, was a florist. I ordered a single, long-stemmed red rose to be delivered to David in the pub at mid-day.

On the stroke of twelve, the doors swung open, and in pranced a burly bloke, singing:

"A, you're adorable; B, you're so beautiful; C, you're a cutie full of charm......"

The men – including David – were laughing hysterically at the performance. When the song was finished, he announced. "Where is David Drew please?" He wasn't laughing now!

The customers cheered and pointed him out, at which, the man opened the gift card and read aloud.
"Roses are red,
Violets are blue,
You're a cantankerous b*****d
But I still love you."

We were little more than a couple of light-hearted love birds when we moved into our first home, and David discovered that he had found a worthy opponent. I was having a shower when he sneaked into the bathroom and threw a mug of ice-cold water over me.

The gloves were off! I waited a few days before taking my revenge. I heard the shower running, waited for him to be off his guard, then hit him with a bucket full of cold water.

He couldn't get his breath, but I didn't feel guilty.

The winters were cold and money was tight in our new home, but we didn't much care. The bedrooms were particularly frosty, having no central heating, so during the cold months, we slept in the lounge.

There was a soft, three-seater sofa, and a green, rock-hard, two-seater. The latter was well-made, old-fashioned, and excruciating. Each night we would argue (often to the point of wrestling), over who would take their turn on the green settee. Being completely in love and each prepared to suffer for the other, we fought, not for the comfy option, but to claim our place on the smaller, lumpier choice. Our mutual stubbornness knew no bounds and often we both slept on the two-seater, squashed together like trampled spiders, neither one prepared to relinquish their place in exchange for a comfortable night if it meant leaving the other to suffer alone.

We have been married for more than thirty years, and my heart still takes a leap when I see him. My soul, it seems, really has found its other half.

Yes, to answer your next question, soulmates do exist. That is not to say, however, that everyone's other half is having a life on earth with them. They could well be in the spirit world, watching you live your life as you make do without them.

Of course, one day you will be reunited, but even if they are here on Earth, there is still the risk that you might pass them by. Those of us who find each other in this confusing, worldly maze, are very fortunate.
When David and I had been together just a few months, a well-known seaside fortune teller approached us after one of David's public demonstrations.

Her demeanor bore a hint of venom, as she curled her lip and sniped that our relationship would not last twelve months. To me, it felt like a blow to the stomach, but David was not the slightest bit disturbed.

He sat with me and explained how it is unprofessional to offer unsolicited information, and that the words of anyone who would blurt out something so hurtful, carried no weight. Many people who profess to be psychic are dishonest. Others, although genuine, have limited ability, and all can make mistakes. It is easy to see if the words of any psychic come from a place of love.

Psychic ability, without spirituality, is a bad combination. This lady appeared to have neither! Spirituality and a desire to help should always go hand in hand with psychic gifts. Anyone who would volunteer such nasty comments does not possess those attributes and should not be taken seriously.

He pointed out that these venomous remarks mean nothing unless you entertain them. If you take them on board, however, they can do real harm. He gave the example that curses have no effect unless you believe in them. It is only the negative feelings they provoke that provide them with any power.

A thought is planted and you unwittingly nurture it, thereby attracting bad things. Like attracts like. It is better to always try to think positively. Negativity can't hurt you if you don't invite it in.

That night, David told me the following story over a glass of home-made beetroot wine he had been sent as a thank-you. (Luckily, he related the story before he lost all sensation in his head. By the end of the bottle, he appeared to be completely sober but felt as though his face was suspended in mid-air, like a mask with nothing behind it. Apparently, beetroot is a natural anesthetic!)

He related how a lady had told him she had seen a tarot card reader some months earlier. He seemed quite professional and told her she was going overseas on holiday. This impressed the woman. It was true, she was about to go on holiday. The reader went on to casually add that while she was there, her husband would have a heart attack and die.

The poor lady was distraught. Every day of their vacation, she was waiting for her husband to collapse. Of course, it didn't happen. Two weeks passed and he was fine, but it ruined their holiday.

David advises that before you visit a medium, you should seek recommendations where possible, and always remember that the future is not fixed. Your current pathway stretches out ahead, but you have your own free will to change direction at any time.

The Little Boy Who Saw Ghosts

When David and I took that first walk in Stanley Park, I couldn't imagine what it would be like to live a life seeing dead people every day. Sensing we could be growing close, I wanted to understand who this man was.

We were passing the rose beds when I ventured to delve a little.

"Have you always seen people in the spirit world? How did it all start?"

We walked, hand in hand, and he raised his eyes to the blue sky. "I don't remember a time when I didn't see them." He lowered his gaze to the path. "When I was a boy, spirit children would visit me. I think I would have been about five. I remember Mary." He smiled. "She used to pop up next to the bed and make me jump. She thought it was hilarious."

I was intrigued.

"Weren't you scared? Most people would be petrified if they saw a dead kid."

"I didn't know she was dead. I guess at five, I didn't really understand what 'dead' was."

"Didn't you wonder how she got into your room, or where she went?"

He paused in thought.

"It never occurred to me. I was just used to it. It was just my normal bedtime routine. I had always seen them."

"You know, all babies are born psychic." He added, "They're fresh from the spirit world themselves. They are more in tune with spirit than with here. Have you never seen a baby cooing up at someone when there's no-one there?"

I admitted that I had.

He nodded. "Usually, when they start to grow up they lose that." He thought for a moment. "That didn't happen with me."

As we approached the lake, the Canada geese were swarming towards us. David went off to buy duck food at the kiosk. They ate noisily, flapping their wings in competition to get the biggest pieces. I waited until the bag was empty and the birds had begun to settle before posing my next question.

"What about your mum and dad? How did they cope with all that?"

He looked wistfully out across the lake. "My dad died when I was very young."

I was embarrassed to have asked, but he continued without breaking his stride.

"Mum thought I had imaginary friends." The memory amused him. "She humoured me at first. I thought everyone could see them. Then I heard her telling my sister I ought to have grown out of it by now." He looked me in the eyes. "It was a shock."

I was trying to take it all in. I felt sympathy for the

kid he had been – and also for his poor mother.
"Was she worried?"
"Oh yeah." He nodded, "She didn't understand it. Especially when I told her Uncle Bill was coming on Sunday. Her face when he actually turned up!" He laughed. "I was only about seven and I had never met him. I got some funny looks that day. Then there was the time Aunt Bessie was pushing me on the swing."

I looked at him enquiringly, waiting for the point of the story. He returned my look.
"She died before I was born." He explained, "Mum dropped the trifle when I told her…. I was gutted! Anyway, she took me to a child-psychiatrist in the end."

I raised my eyebrows. "What did *he* say?"
David shrugged. "Turned out he was a widower. I could see his wife in the room, so I just told him what she looked like and what she wanted to say. After that, he told my mum he didn't understand it, and to take me away."

This was fascinating stuff, but I could see David was tiring of the inquisition, so I let it go. It seemed to me he wanted to be a normal guy, not a freak show. He wanted me to love him for who he was, not what he could do. This was something I knew I could do, but I was still curious about what life was like for him; what emotionally supporting him would involve.

To this day, David rarely wants to talk about work when he is relaxing. I suppose this is the same for most people. The nature of his gift, however, does dictate some interference from time to time.

For example, we have been at restaurants when a lady in spirit wants him to give a message to her daughter on the next table. He won't do this. You never know if the person would be receptive to the situation or if they would become upset. Unsolicited messages are off the menu, so to speak. Once, a respectable-looking man of about forty, took a table for one. He seemed perfectly amenable, but David pointed out that he was agitated and could be quite volatile.
"Really? He looks fine to me."
"His aura is blood red. He's angry."

Before our coffee could be served, sure enough, he was shouting down the phone at someone, brandishing his breadstick like an offensive weapon.

However, as a rule, work and play are not a good mix. I soon found that David would rather go for a pint at the end of the day than talk about the spirit world, which was a frustration in the beginning when I was thirsty for it all, but I tried to be patient, and slowly came to learn more about the background of the little boy who saw ghosts.

As I became more integrated into his world, I realised that the majority of spiritual mediums seem to develop one, or maybe two psychic abilities as adults.

It was apparent that David was different. Like the little boy from the movie Sixth Sense, he had his gifts thrust on him, like it or not.

He is what is known as a natural medium, who started his life, so to speak, with a foot in each world.

Those of you who have read David's autobiography, *'The Other Side; a Psychic's Story'*, will know that he had very humble beginnings.

After the death of his father, David's mother, Joan - a diminutive but feisty Welsh lady, was left to bring up her brood of four children alone. David was the youngest, his brother Tim being his closest sibling. Their older sisters, Helen and Annette, helped look after the boys while their mum went out to work, cleaning at the local hospital.

It was a struggle for the single mum to keep the family afloat. There were few luxuries, but David remembers the lasting effect the kindness of others had on him.

At nursery, there was free school milk, and a chocolate biscuit wrapped in foil for those who had sixpence. David never had any money, however, and would watch with wide eyes as the other children enjoyed their treats.

One day the teacher called him out to the front of the class. She told him there was a spare biscuit and asked him if he would like it.
When he told me this story, it was with the hindsight that his teacher must have paid for the biscuit herself.

He was still touched by this more than twenty years later, although I'm sure she forgot it long ago. It struck me that the smallest of kind acts can have a bigger impact than you might imagine.

Christmas time in the Drew household was a particularly stressful time for David's mum. Having barely enough money to keep the children clothed and fed, his mother had no money for gifts for the children. Listening to him reminisce made me realise how privileged my childhood had been. We were far from wealthy, but I was always well provided for. I felt a pang of guilt listening to David's stories.

One year the milk-man, who could see that the family was struggling, left a stack of presents on the doorstep with the milk. David remembers the year when he was given a tricycle and a cowboy outfit, although not until years later did he learn of their secret benefactor.

Perhaps the influence of this generosity contributed to David, as an adult, adopting various small causes of his own. Years later, when he heard that a small local boy had his bike stolen, he bought him a new one, and when he read in the newspaper that a single mum was burgled just before Christmas, leaving her with no presents for the children, he sent money to replace them. It pleases him to do these things, even at times when he can't afford it.

In the 1990s we started Scarlet Ribbons (named for the song where the parent is heartbroken because their daughter has asked only for ribbons, and they are unable to find any). We worked to solicit contributions from local shops and other generous donors to give Santa a hand and provide gifts for families who were in hardship.

David always says that the way to find happiness is to make other people happy. I can vouch for that.

Psychic ability, in David's case, didn't run in the family. It seems his visions and predictions were an unexpected baptism of fire for the bewildered Drew household.

He relates fond memories of summer days, down at the bottom of the garden, when spirit children would play with him, hiding in the shadows of the natural den formed by the willow tree. They would tell him how they used to be poorly and he would invent imaginary ailments, so as not to feel left out.

I was intrigued as to what happens to children when they die. David explained they are looked after in the spirit world, often by a close family member. They learn, develop and have their childhood, much as they would have done on earth. They play with other spirit children, and sometimes with children on the earth. They are regularly taken to visit the parents they left behind. When people come to see him, it is not unusual for them to be accompanied by their unseen son or daughter.

In his boyhood days, David longed to be like his spirit

friends, but in his teenage years, he tried to ignore them, wanting to be normal and fit-in with his school pals, a habit he would perfect over the years to come. David's bedtime visitors were not just children. He told me about a monk and one very different visitor whose appearance baffled him.

One night as he was falling asleep, a beautiful young woman, surrounded by a cloud of gold and silver light appeared by his bed. He was overwhelmed at the sight, and his first childish thought was that she must be an angel. Then she introduced herself as Patricia - his sister. Confused, he politely told her she was mistaken; that his sisters, Helen and Annette, were asleep in the next room. She smiled knowingly, then disappeared.

The next morning over breakfast, David mentioned his unusual visitor to his mum and Tim. Of course, they were accustomed to hearing about his spiritual experiences, but this one drew a response he did not expect. His mum burst into tears.

Her reaction played on his mind all day in school. He was worried about his mum; confused at what he had done to upset her.

When he came home from school, his mum, having composed herself, sat the boys down for a serious chat. She told them that her first baby, a little girl, had been stillborn, many years before. They named her Patricia.

She had grown in the spirit world and was obviously watching over her little brother.

These must have been worrying times for Joan Drew. Where do you go to get advice if your son is seeing dead people?

Help did come when the time was right, in the form of an apparently random meeting. It seems there are no coincidences.

The afternoon was rainy, and two small ladies, sheltering at the bus-stop, struck up a conversation. They chatted for a while, then the first lady, David's mum, opened up about her youngest son. She was concerned by his strange premonitions and visions. The second lady, who was named Mrs. Woolley, was president of the local Spiritualist Church. She completely understood all of David's experiences and was able to reassure his mum, and offered to help.

When Joan arrived home, soaking wet but elated, she told David about her meeting. Later that week they accepted Mrs. Woolley's invitation and visited with her at her home.

The house was modest but immaculate. David said it was homely, and fondly remembered the china cups she always used. She chatted with his mum, and at that first meeting, he wasn't sure why they were there.

Suddenly she spoke to him directly. "I can see an

Indian Chief next to you, David."

Now she had his attention. He had never known of anyone else who could see people who were in spirit. It was exciting. At last, someone understood.

They spoke for some time, exchanging details of what they saw and heard, as his poor mother listened in amazement.

Mrs. Woolley and David were to become close, if unlikely friends. David said that she took him under her wing, teaching him the names of the gifts of clairvoyance (seeing), clairaudience (hearing), spiritual healing, clairsentience (feeling), and trance-mediumship (more on this later). He learned that psychometry is where information is transferred from a given object to the holder and is an art to be developed, rather than a natural gift.

She would make strawberry flans for him, and always had a pot of tea ready when he came around after school. She invited him to join her weekly circle of regular sitters from the church. They would sit to communicate with the spirit world, in what you or I would call a séance. Now he had allies; other people who understood him. They were an unlikely mix; adult men and women – mostly elderly, and a teenage schoolboy, but they were on the same wavelength, and they were all amazed at the extent of this young boy's remarkable talent.

By the time David was fourteen, he was taking

services at the Spiritualist Church, passing on messages from the rostrum.

When we met, I had never heard of a Spiritualist Church. David explained that it is just like a normal church, with prayers and hymns, but a guest medium passes on messages from loved ones in spirit at some point during the service.

His mum, no longer worried, saw how amazed the congregation were, and was extremely proud of him. She would stand at the church door as they left, telling everyone in turn, "That's my son!"

Suddenly, the very thing that David had tried to hide, was something to be proud of. Everyone was eager to see the boy David, and wanted to know what, and who he saw with them. He told me he would come home to find his mother making tea for people who had turned up in the hope of having a reading from him.

As a boy, David helped his mum out financially by working a paper-round, and later a job in a butcher's shop after school. As a young adult, he would see people in the evenings for readings and healing and would hold public demonstrations, as and when he had the time.

He told me that as he grew older, he came to realise he had been given his gifts for a reason, and that it was his duty to be using them more. His spirit guide was pushing for him to do this work full time, which is all well and good, but on Earth people need to eat!

David told me how he wrestled with this for a while. He knew that if he was going to do this, he would need to charge people for his services. He didn't really want to do that. His inner conflict ended when he came to realise that even vicars, priests, and other vocational workers get paid. There and then he decided to work full-time as a psychic medium.

He would be able to dedicate his life to showing people that their loved ones were living on and that how they live this life is very important. He would not be ashamed to charge, but vowed never to turn anyone away if they needed help but couldn't afford to pay.

Around the time we met, David had a very active lifestyle. He would play football and lift weights regularly.

Once, when we visited my dad, I forgot my key. David was very athletic, and managed to scale the patio doors and enter through the tiny top window. Other aspects of his habits, however, could certainly have been healthier. He smokes heavily, likes his fried food, and consumes copious amounts of caffeine.

Whenever I tried to convert him, over the years, he would shrug and tell me he wasn't afraid of dying.

I think he overlooked the issue that dying wasn't the only potential consequence, but that his quality of life could be seriously compromised by his habits.

The first signs of this were insidious. David was in his forties and had just written, *Stairway to Heaven*. His work was relentless, and we were enjoying a much-needed holiday on the Algarve when I first noticed that he was struggling with pain in his legs.

If I wanted to visit a market, for example, he would suggest waiting for me in a coffee shop. Slowly I noticed he wanted to stop and rest at every café. We adjusted our lifestyle to allow for this, and it simply became the new normal. I tried to coax him into seeing a doctor, but, ever stubborn, he refused.

Life went on as his work took off.

Bumps in the Night

I am married to a man who is more terrified of bees than of ghosts; who will cower in a thunderstorm but happily face a poltergeist.

Paranormal activity surrounds him daily. Over the years, I have become somewhat desensitised to this. The spirit world is all around us, concealed behind the thinnest of veils, a mere dimension away. When you live with a man who has a foot in each camp, you can expect to experience a little crossover. I don't flinch anymore at the occasional face peering around a door, or footsteps on the stairs, but it would be untrue to say I have never had any heart-lurching moments.

Death is historically depicted as a thing to be feared, whether an Egyptian, jackal-headed god or the scythe bearing grim-reaper. In every horror film or thriller, you will find a protagonist striving to escape the jaws of death, but is it really such a terrible thing? I suppose the answer depends on the kind of life you have led. I am not afraid of death, although I hope for a peaceful rather than a painful passing. I have had more blessings in this life than I am worthy of. What comes after, good or bad, will be exactly what I deserve.

We should all reconcile with this because it is how we live our life which determines our circumstance in the worlds to come.

Not much is promised in this life, but be sure we will all eventually die. Hopefully, this will be after a long and productive life, and for most of us, it will not be the worst thing we experience. Death is not the end of the world – at least, it is only the end of this one. No-one wants to die a horrible, painful death, but the act of passing over is a simple matter of nature. Its dread is born from a lack of understanding. The classic cliché; 'fear of the unknown'.

When I think back to when I've been truly afraid, two occasions immediately raise their heads. I'm not sure, however, if I should count the first in the exclusive experiences of a psychic's wife. We were renting a holiday cottage in Devon, at the time, which was quite obviously haunted. I'm sure that anyone would have clearly seen the same terrifying apparition I did that evening.

As a bit of background, I should explain that for many years, David held psychic development circles. They were designed to help people nurture their inner psychic abilities. I sat regularly, as did our daughter Ayesha, who at fourteen, was the only one of our three children old enough to participate at that time. These classes serve to make people more aware of the spirit world around them.

Sitters gradually learn to open themselves up to those

from other dimensions and become receptive to their influence, but of everything I observed in these classes, nothing alarmed me like my experience that night in Devon.

We had booked our stay in what truly was a beautiful, thatched cottage, nestling right on the edge of Dartmoor. Built circa 1833, it was the stuff of picture postcards. Roses around the door; bird-bath in the garden and fully furnished Welsh-dresser. Amid the homely horse-brasses and toby-jugs, the atmosphere was warm and relaxing. You can tell by the feel of a place if there is anything malevolent there. There was the underlying buzz of paranormal activity, but nothing negative. Perfect for the Drew family, it was a pleasant, if somewhat other-worldly vibe.

At night in the bedroom, David's sleep was often disturbed by the hum of invisible women lost in whispered conversation. Nice ladies, and happy enough. No need to try to move them on. After all, we were the intruders in this house. There were a couple of small, spirit dogs too. I would feel them jump onto the couch and settle into the crook of my knees in the evenings. This is not what unnerved me. It was actually rather nice. Playing in the garden one day, our younger daughter Sian, disturbed some long grass to reveal two mini gravestones, placed to the memory of these once-loved pets.

Once or twice, while in the bathroom, the kids saw a face at the frosted glass window, which did spook them a bit - largely because it was eight–feet off the ground and distorted by the glass, but they knew their dad would look after them when it came to anything spooky. They even called on him in dreams if they were having a nightmare and needed to be rescued.

(I taught them this trick after trying it myself. When I shouted him, David would appear in the periphery of my dream, and I knew I was safe.)

Then, one night, events in the cottage took a dramatic turn. The children were in bed and I had stayed up to take in the end of a film. David had turned in uncharacteristically early, as he was feeling off-colour with the fledgling symptoms of a cold. I curled up on the chintzy sofa, eating my Turkish delight by the light of the television, determined to finish the movie. To my left, the hall door stood open in the dark, as did the dining-room door beyond.

About twenty minutes in, I was disturbed by a bright light in my peripheral vision. I spun around and turned ice-cold. There was a dazzling, slow-moving orb; chest height, and about the size of a dinner plate. It was as though someone was carrying a lamp, but all I could see was the light.

As I stared, wide-eyed, fully expecting it to disappear, it immerged from the direction of the kitchen and moved into the dining room. Then it turned and slowly advanced toward me. There I was, this hard-core wife of a ghostbuster - absolutely petrified!

With hindsight, I don't really know why this particular apparition frightened me so disproportionately.

The vibe was not malicious. Perhaps it was the fact that I didn't know who was there, (someone earthbound perhaps?) or maybe because it was such a tangible, objective experience, coupled with my being alone, cut off from my personal saviour and exorcist.

The entity navigated the dining-room table as I helplessly watched, before entering the hallway. Pausing for a moment, it then crossed the lobby and hovered in the doorway of my room, only three feet or so from where I sat. It was so bright, I could see nothing beyond it. The halo around the light filled the width of the door frame. I was frozen to the spot, as ten long seconds ticked past on the loud, mantel clock. It felt as though someone was staring back at me. I was sure they could see me. Why else had they stopped? I wondered if they would come in. Then, to my relief, the orb turned sharply and went upstairs.

My heart was banging in my ears. I couldn't care less about the film at this point. I just wanted to go to bed – be with David, my protector. But there were logistical problems. I had to follow it upstairs to reach the bedroom! Some time passed before I summoned the courage to do so. Thankfully, by then the coast was clear, and our spiritual hostess (I felt it was probably a lady) was gone from sight.

My second memorable fright happened at home, early one summer evening.

At that time we were living in a three-story, Victorian

property, which, when we moved in, was already occupied by several spiritual squatters. The predominant character was a pretty young lady in floor-length, flowing gown. David would often see her smiling up from the parquet floor at the foot of the sweeping staircase. She seemed quite content, and her presence, only ever mentioned in passing, was not an issue for us. After all, we have always been only one step removed from the Adams Family.

People in spirit are around us all. Departed friends and family, once they have settled into their home in the spirit world, can visit with their loved ones on Earth.

Then there are the 'ghosts', who tend to hang around; usually attached to a place rather than a person. There can be a variety of reasons for this. Some don't realise they are dead and retain an earthly attachment to a certain location. Others just have problems moving on. Perhaps they are troubled by something they feel has been left unfinished and are reluctant to leave.

Strange things would often happen in that house, but nothing I would class as scary. The TV would mysteriously change channel when we left the room, and the light-pull in the bathroom would periodically be found stretched across the high ceiling, dangling down through the centre of light-shade. Once or twice a month we would have to fetch ladders to set it right, so the kids didn't have to bathe in the dark.

We engaged one or two babysitters who were freaked out by these happenings. The detached gravestone propped against the garden wall didn't help, but these were just standard, every-day situations for members of the Drew household.

Twice, when I was making a cup of tea in the kitchen at bedtime, David's shaving mirror leapt from where it was propped against the wall at the back of the counter, dropping face down in the middle of the floor before my eyes. (It may have continued to happen, except on the second occasion, it shattered.) I thought this was great! It was exciting that they were able to physically move stuff. Again, the vibes were all good. Interesting rather than frightening.

On the evening in question, David decided he was going out to the local pub. Never much of a party-girl, I stayed home with the children, my bed-socks, and the TV remote.

It was an old house, with little or no security. The large, sash windows could be easily breached, and despite the relatively low crime rate in our area, David was over-protective when it came to the 'living', and gave me a safety check-list before setting out.

"Keep the door locked. Don't answer it to anyone. Here's the pub's number. Phone me if there is a problem."

He kissed me goodbye and I carried on washing the

dishes. The kids were upstairs, feeding their Tamagotchi and putting on their pyjamas. A blackbird sang lazily in the garden. All was well with the world.

My chores almost done for the night, I dried my hands and picked up the milk bottles, embracing them in my arms as I heaved open the heavy front door. Already bending, I reached to place them on the step - and there I saw the legs and waist of a man. He momentarily startled me, then I laughed at my own foolishness. As I moved to straighten up, his folded arms were in my line of sight, and above that – nothing. He disappeared.

I closed the door, taken aback somewhat, but not afraid. Then I began to think. Who *was* that? Why was he there? He stood, legs apart, arms folded, like he intended to deliberately scare me; scold me even. But why? It's not a nice thing to do. The more I thought about it, the more I concluded that this was someone with bad intent; someone up to no good. And also, he had vanished before I saw his face. When I dwelt on these details, I became increasingly uneasy. I was on edge all evening until at last, I heard David's key in the door.

It was just after midnight when he returned; a happy and carefree man. I hurriedly made him a coffee, anxious to spit out the details of my fright and recount the evening's events. I placed the mug beside him and gave him an account of my evening.
"There was something about his stance;" I told him, finishing my story, "legs astride; arms folded."

David turned on the television and I eagerly awaited his explanation.

One advantage of being married to a psychic is that when something scary happens, you have someone who can protect you; reassure you; make it all go away. Wouldn't you think?

I was less than happy with his response.

"That's good."

"Good? What's good about it? I've been petrified all night! Who was it?"

"I left someone on the door to look after you." He spoke absent-mindedly as he surfed through the channels. "Sounds like he did a good job. To be fair, I did tell you not to open it. What's for supper?"

If you will indulge me, I feel the need to digress here, to briefly explain something that will provide a little context. It is easy to take the workings of spirit for granted when you spend the day engaging with dead people, forgetting that this is new territory for some, as it once was for me.

Forgive me if you have read David's books, *'Stairway to Heaven,'* and *'The Other Side; A Psychic's Story.'* as you will already be familiar with the following.

We all have one spirit guide and several spirit helpers. They watch over us, discreetly trying to influence us to do the right thing, to take the right path, and generally not bugger things up.

Some people think of this in terms of their conscience.

Our guide is with us from the moment we are born until we pass over, and for a little while after. They make it their mission to get us through this life and out the other side safely.

My Dad was born in 1927. When he was three years old, he was sitting on the rug, playing with his toys. Suddenly, in the doorway, he saw a Zulu warrior. The man, who appeared huge to the little boy, ran towards him and disappeared.

My dad began to cry inconsolably. His mum scooped him up and tried to comfort him, but he didn't have the words to describe what he had seen. Living in a 1930's English village, he had never seen a person of colour. With no TV, and being too young to read, he hadn't even seen pictures of anyone dressed like this. And how could a three-year-old explain how someone vanished? Throughout his seventy years, he never forgot this. I wonder now if the man was his guide or perhaps a helper.

Helpers come and go, popping in and out of our lives as and when they are needed. Most people are completely unaware of this, but David's entourage are *very* present and frequently make their presence felt

I am not afraid of these guys. They are as much a part of our household as our earthly family members.

Despite the fact they are all of high spiritual standing, their personalities differ immensely. So, life with a medium can feel a little crowded at times. Here is a condensed cast list of some of the usual suspects who share our personal space.

Blue Cloud is David's spirit guide and my dear friend. I hope you didn't choke on your custard cream. I know this sounds weird. I am acutely aware that normal people don't talk to Native American chiefs who have been dead for four hundred years, but to us and to our children, he is one of the family, involved in and witness to, many aspects of our day-to-day life.

My own spirit guide was a Spanish nun named Maria. I feel her close to me daily, in a subjective way. I know that I owe her a lot. The best of me is down to her, and I have learned to try to take a moment, when faced with decisions, to allow for her inspiration.

David's spirit entourage are in more direct communication, however, and Blue Cloud, or BC as we have come to call him, is a very special friend. David has conversed with him since childhood, and for my part, I count myself honoured to have the opportunity to speak with him personally from time to time. David occasionally assumes trance-state, allowing BC to use his body for communication purposes. (More on this later.)

A powerful man, Blue Cloud's appearance is overwhelming. David once estimated him to stand at around six feet seven-inches tall. He shows himself at various ages, but claims to have lived to be one hundred and twenty-four. (David is sceptical of this. He is convinced that he is measuring time in what he disrespectfully refers to as 'cat years'.)

BC wears a full, feathered headdress, or occasionally a narrow-rimmed, black hat with a small plume. (The Indian Chief who the man saw with me at that first psychic demonstration, now has more credibility. I have since learned that this was Blue Cloud, working his magic to try to bring us together.) His expression tends to be serious, although he does have a kind heart and a sense of humour. (David would contest this last point, never having seen him laugh.) It can seem comical, however when he attempts, in broken English, to use some modern-day phrase or idiom.

He has, from time to time, indulged the inquirer with various personal details about himself, but he prefers to speak on a higher, more spiritual vein. Past lives having limited appeal to him.

At first meeting, he can seem overpowering and stern, but he is wise, sincere, compassionate, and empathetic; like one who has experienced great sorrow and wants to help others avoid it. I feel his presence often; both his love and his reproach, but although he inspires awe, I could never be afraid of him.

Blue Cloud first made his presence felt when David was around ten. In bed one night in his tiny box-room, balanced on the edge of sleep, David was startled by a loud bang, and the room filled with an explosion of light. When his eyes grew accustomed to the glow, he saw a huge North American Indian Chief in full battle dress, standing by his wardrobe.

It was an intimidating sight for a small boy, but although he was overwhelmed, he instinctively knew his character was kindly.

The big man introduced himself to the boy David and told him he was there to guide him, and that he had always been with him.

After that night, David often saw Blue Cloud as he went about his day. He learned that they could communicate telepathically, which spared any embarrassment on the walk to school.

BC would often appear with words of encouragement or advice, both welcome and unwelcome, and when David felt he needed him, there he would be, like his very own genie in the lamp.

David is occasionally asked why spirit guides are always North American Indians. Of course, they are not, but it is true, many guides did originate from this culture, especially the guides of spiritual mediums.

This is because they were, by nature, a spiritual race even before they passed over. They spoke to their forefathers and regularly communed with the Sacred Spirit. Their earthly beliefs stand them in good stead, often giving them a head-start on the spiritual ladder, which makes them, and others from similarly spiritually-minded cultures, perfect candidates for the job. You can see perhaps how a merchant banker might not be quite at the appropriate point in their spiritual journey to take on this role.

Blue Cloud was not always a Native American chief, however. He had other lives and could show himself as he appeared in any of these. A person's last incarnation is their usual choice however and so it is with BC.

The usual reason for reincarnation, is to help a person progress spiritually. We can learn a lot from the experiences gained by having another life on earth. It is the return to innocence. All previous mistakes are forgotten, and you start over with a clean slate and the precious gift of a chance to do better. The trouble is, we have no recollection of what we did wrong the last time we were here, or what, specifically, we need to improve upon. Our guides in the spirit world try to coax us in the right direction, but sadly, are often ignored.

There are exceptions, however. Some people come back, not so much to learn as to teach us something.

No one is forced to have another life on Earth, and usually, the equivalent of hundreds of years pass between each incarnation. It would be very unusual for a person to pass to spirit and find that someone they were close to had already been reincarnated.

Bart and Yeung are two of David's spirit helpers. Unlike Blue Cloud, they are not always with him, but rather come and go as required. Bart is peaceful and pious by nature and is of Jewish heritage. He shows himself to be robed in plain, coarse fabric. His hair, eyes and beard are dark, and when he speaks, he is forthright and truthful, sometimes brutally so. He doesn't spare the emotional rod to spoil the child, but he always acts with love. I am not afraid of him, but I sometimes fear his relentless honesty which holds a mirror to my faults.

Yeung is a gentle and unassuming man, whose last incarnation was somewhere in China. He shows himself with a long, grey beard and a soft smile. In life, he was an early medical pioneer, who specialized in conditions relating to the head, ears, and eyes. We rarely hear from him, but his presence, when felt, is serene. He prefers to play his part from behind the scenes, remaining modest and inconspicuous.

One spirit helper who is not shy to make his presence felt, is Pepe. In life, he was a clown who fell to his death from a tightrope in full view of a huge crowd during a circus performance. An acrobat had fallen from the trapeze. As she was attended to, the clowns were sent in to distract the crowd.

Pepe climbed the rigging for an impromptu display, and walked the tightrope, as he had done many times before, but this time it ended in tragedy.

The sad fact that his death was witnessed by many

people, including the children he was hoping to entertain, remains painful to him, hundreds of years later.

He is around a metre tall and wears white-face make-up, sporting the traditional red nose, black bowler hat, and a red, squirty flower. His high-pitched laugh and comic façade, disguise a sensitivity and wisdom which are easily overlooked, and should not be underestimated.

As a boy, when David was playing football, he would catch sight of this little Italian clown running up and down the side-lines. Throughout his life, Pepe has been there to help lift David's spirits and influence him to cheer people up, when they need it.

Those early days of living with David were a sharp learning curve. It's strange now to think back to when this was all new to me.

We would be falling asleep at night when suddenly, I would feel someone sit on the bed, or see a wardrobe door open. I would instantly be wide awake!
"Who is that? Who's there?"
David wouldn't open his eyes.
"I don't know. I'm asleep."

He didn't appreciate being disturbed by them - or by me. He was off the clock, and could not be coaxed. These days I am equally undisturbed by such experiences, but I still remember the days when these nightly visitors were new and alarming.

One evening, we were watching TV in the lounge, when David passed some tongue-in-cheek remark to Pepe, who replied to this banter by rattling the cutlery in the kitchen drawer. David laughed and didn't bat an eye. Now, because I was with David and therefore knew who was playing tricks, I wasn't afraid. However, I sat there, wide-eyed, completely oblivious to the drama playing out on Coronation Street, then wandered into the kitchen (after a respectable interval), to casually check on the knives and forks. I still have no idea what I was expecting to find.

Another of Pepe's habits was to run around upstairs, especially when the baby was sleeping. We would hear quick, heavy steps from the bedroom above our heads. In the early days, I would go up, just to check for intruders. In the end, I took no notice. Visiting guests however, were a little freaked out by these antics. I think Pepe just enjoyed spending time with the kids.

In later years, when we left the children with babysitters, Pepe would stay home with them and cause mayhem. At the age of five, our daughter Sian described him perfectly when she looked up with her chocolate button eyes and told us about the funny little man who had been making her laugh the night before.

The children had no fear of our spirit friends. They grew up with them. When they were poorly, Uncle Albert, as they call the spirit doctor who helps David, would give them healing and make them better.

It was always so natural to them, in contrast to David's childhood, where he was the only family member who was aware of the spirit world, thus causing his family some noticeable concern for a while.

Our children, however, had no concept that other houses did not have a healing-bed or spirit lodgers. They didn't realise that it was probably best not to talk to their friends and teachers about Uncle Albert and the gang. To them, it was just every-day life.

I recall our eldest girl, Ayesha, at the end of term, bringing home an English book filled with essays about Blue Cloud and how she wanted to be a spirit guide when she grew up – or a duck.

It was a great school, and nothing was ever said - not even about the duck! Being a church school, however, we did receive a visit one summer from the local vicar, who was putting out feelers after hearing that David was a professional psychic. (He was so often in the local papers and on radio or TV, we could not have kept it quiet, even if we wanted to.) When the Reverend arrived, he seemed surprised to see a house filled with religious icons and Christian artifacts from our trip to Jerusalem.

After a cup of tea and a chat, he decided that we were not the spawn of the devil he was expecting, and promptly called off the exorcism.

A lot of clergymen decry the practice of talking with

the dead. It stems from a fear of what they don't understand, and, to be fair, there are a lot of con men and women out there.

These people give genuine mediums a bad name. The times David and I have shared an eye-roll when some charlatan is depicted on TV, knowing how all psychics get tarred with the same brush. However, as there are accounts in the bible of Jesus talking with the dead, perhaps priests shouldn't be so quick to call it the devil's work.

For example, if you turn to Matthew 17:1 you will find an account of the disciples climbing up a mountain with Jesus and witnessing him speaking with Moses and Elijah, both dead for hundreds of years.

In addition to David's helpers, there are, of course, many others in the spirit world who seek him out. Mostly they are hoping to use him as an instrument of communication, much like a telephone, to pass messages on to their loved ones.

He can't call anyone up, however, any more than your mobile can decide for itself who to dial. Often, people come to see him hoping for a message from a specific person.

If the person is there and able to communicate, that's great, but if it is someone else who is with them at that moment, there is nothing he can do. He is just a facilitating instrument - albeit one that would like to turn itself off from time to time.

Some aspects of David's work have the potential to be scary, for example, when people come for help after a bad experience with the Ouija board, or when he is called upon to rid people's homes of poltergeists. These entities make their presence known by throwing objects or moving things around. While it is true that ghosts can't hurt you, being hit on the head by a flying ornament can certainly do some damage!

Having the ability to see who is there, and ask them why they are acting out, David is able, with the help of Blue Cloud, to guide them over to where they belong. He maintains he has a responsibility to help, not only the victim of the haunting but also the spirit entity. This serves the person in spirit, as well as the petrified victim, and is usually fairly straightforward.

Poltergeists are rarely malevolent, and usually, a little coaxing in the right direction is all that is needed. It is often some poor old dear who doesn't understand that she has died, and perhaps throws things at the new occupants of her house, thinking them to be intruders.

An abundance of psychic energy enables the person in spirit to move solid objects.

This is why it is common for an adolescent to be in residence where there is an issue with poltergeist activity, as they often generate an excess of energy which can be utilised, rather like a battery.

(Not to be confused with telekinesis, where it is the teenagers themselves who inadvertently uses the energy to move objects.)

Usually, a tactful conversation and a glimpse of their destination, is enough to persuade the entity to move on. However, when the spirit is less congenial, a more forceful approach may be required from David and his spirit helpers.

The strange case of the King's Head pub in Egremont springs to mind as an appropriate example.

It started one morning when the tenants woke to find a twelve-inch knife protruding from their kitchen wall. Gradually the incidents gathered pace. The next day, the oven turned itself on, and another time, they found the room awash with water, with all the taps running.

It came to a head one night time when the couple awoke in the dark to the sound of papers rustling in their bedroom. After this, they decided to seek help.
As the husband made the call to David, his wife cried out in the background. Her Celtic cross had become red-hot and scorched her neck.

David travelled to the Lake District to assess the situation in person. When he arrived, the pub was open and busy. The couple explained their experiences, then he was discretely shown to the cellar, where a Celtic cross inside a kite shape had mysteriously been mapped out on the floor in salt.

Within moments of opening the heavy door, he saw the problem. From the cellar steps, he was looking down on a skinny, balding figure, surrounded by a swirling mist. It was like looking through black lace. The man stared angrily back at him with dark eyes. This was no confused old dear, and it was not going to be easy. As David stared back at the shadowy figure, he felt a rope tightening at his throat. Then the cellar walls morphed into prison cell-like structures. This was an earthbound character who had been hanged many years ago and had no desire to leave. Getting him to cross over would certainly be a challenge.

Undeterred, David closed his eyes and prayed. He sensed Blue Cloud beside him, and through closed eyelids, he saw a light growing brighter. When he opened them, the man's expression had turned to fear. There was a blinding flash, and he was gone, whisked off to where he belonged, with the help of David and his friends.

If you have read '*The Other Side; A Psychic's Story*', you will recall how actor, Ricky Tomlinson, called on David to sort out a stubborn poltergeist or two of his own.

It was after his Brookside days, but before he starred in Cracker and The Royle Family, and at that time he was running a casting agency and The Limelight club in Liverpool.
One evening, a friend of his was taken ill at the club, so Ricky said she could lie down upstairs.

After a short while, there was a crash and a series of screams.

He ran up to the room, taking two steps at a time, and found her clinging to a small, ornamental balcony.

In terror she had smashed the window with a chair and climbed out onto the ledge, less afraid of the drop than of the ghostly man who was blocking her exit, shouting wildly that he was waiting for Nellie.

Two days later a regular customer at the club passed away. Her name was Nellie.

There were other strange happenings; a lady on the spiral staircase would appear, then disappear half way down; voices were heard in empty rooms; pool balls rolled around on their own and lights would turn off and on without any explanation.

It took a few visits from David to weigh up the situation and decide how best to approach it. I went with him one time.

My abiding memory of that iron staircase is the horrific, oppressive atmosphere. There was a sense that we were in the presence of something particularly nasty.

For the first time ever, I was afraid for David. He had arranged to go up there alone and confront whatever entities were in residence.

I was confident he could handle it, but this intense level of malevolence made me apprehensive; like I was watching him walk into battle.

David wandered the darkened, upstairs corridors with Blue Cloud at his side. He explored the upper floors, moving from room to room, eyeing the shadows and waiting for someone to make contact, but all was quiet but for the occasional creak. At last, in the doorway to a bathroom, a tall, strongly built figure in a long grey coat materialized. His menacing stare was fixed on David, as a rumbling noise formed into a shout, and erupted with a northern Irish twang.
"When I get my hands on him…I'm gonna KILL HIM!"

Suddenly, a barrage of plastic bleach and shampoo bottles flew out of the bathroom towards David, who instinctively raised his arms to shield his face. When he lowered them, he could see a smaller, unkempt man in a shadowy corner. He looked unshaven and scrawny, with greasy hair falling across his face. In a matter of moments, David was shown the story. The disheveled man had shot the big guy in a gangland-style confrontation some years ago when the building had been a gentleman's club. Decades later the feud still raged, and the hatred between these characters was electric.

Blue Cloud was not prepared to take any more chances with David's safety.

In a flash of white light, the two displaced spirits were whisked away, leaving the hallway dark and quiet at last.

David and Ricky became friends, and once or twice, David held evenings of clairvoyance at the Limelight. Some footage of these nights can be seen on YouTube.

When people meddle with Ouija boards, it is even more frightening, because ordinary people open doors they cannot close on a world they can't understand. The result can be catastrophic.

David always advises people to steer clear of this practice, not because the boards don't work, but because they can attract all kinds of strange characters in spirit. Not everyone is a nice person. There are a lot of shady people on this earth, and they die too. You wouldn't let them into your home now, and you shouldn't let them in when they are dead.

Just because someone is dead, it doesn't mean they have all the answers. The act of passing over won't turn a fool into a wise man, or a criminal into a saint. Those on the high spirit planes can help and advise, but there are many lower planes, where even the well-meaning don't necessarily have much idea.

The concept, originally scribbled letters and an upturned glass, is an ancient one. 1891 saw an incredibly irresponsible marketing venture in

America, produce a commercial version of this talking board, after it had been proven to work and the patent approved.

It made its way to the UK and into my family home in the 1970s, when my teenage brother received one as a gift. It consisted of a wooden board marked with letters, and a heart-shaped plastic planchette with a clear window.

The board spells out its message, but without the presence of a medium, you can't see who is communicating with you. This opens you up to a whole other-world of trouble.

If your electrics were on the blink, you wouldn't start poking around blindly, you would find a good electrician. The same principle applies. Go to a well-recommended medium, don't play with the Ouija board. You would not believe how often it ends badly. I couldn't count the number of times David has been called on to help someone who is being hounded by some kind of spiritual stalker, having attached themselves to the person after a drunken experiment with the Ouija board.

I remember having a conversation with one such girl who was waiting to see David. She was telling me that, since she had used the Ouija board, taps would turn off mid-shower, the plug would be pulled out of the bath, and clothes on hangers moved away from her hand when she reached for them.

She was terrified. As she spoke, I looked around and realised that she had no regard for her audience.

Beside her sat a woman, who had come for a standard reading. Her eyes were growing wider and wider as she tried to appear au-fait with the situation. At last, the girl finished talking and turned to the poor lady, who remarked, as though it was an everyday occurrence, "Yeah. It's rotten when that happens."

Having stressed that I in no way recommend this practice, now for my confession.
I have used the Ouija board myself.

It was in the years before I met David; before I saw first-hand the damage it can do. I was very lucky to escape largely unscathed - apart from being scared half to death.

As a teenager, I found the battered box in a storage cupboard at home, and managed to convince my mum to have a go. We sat in the lounge, closed our eyes, and placed our finger-tips on the pointer. A dim lamp was lit and the curtains were closed.

We sat in silence. At first, nothing happened, but then the planchette began to move – slowly at first then gathering momentum. Mum laughed. "You are pushing it!"
I wasn't.

The movements were smooth and swift, with abrupt

stops and changes in direction, as it indicated a series of seemingly random letters. I removed one hand to write them down. The pointer kept moving as we watched, wide-eyed.

Having heard the theory that participants can subconsciously push the pointer, which is a distinct possibility, I set an experiment. I told my mum to close her eyes tight and turn her head so that she couldn't see the letters.

As the pointer continued to move, I gently lifted my own fingers. The pointer moved faster and Mum laughed. "You're pushing it!" She opened her eyes and her face changed. My hands were by my side.

Taking a break, we examined the string of letters I had written, and realised that, if we divided them in the right places, there were words.
GOTOCHURCH   JOEISHAPPY   IKNOWYOU

It was a series of about twelve short phrases, which didn't mean much to us, but they had miraculously formed, partially while we chatted or had our eyes closed. We resumed our positions, resolving to find out who was there. I asked the question, aware that the answer might not be truthful.
"What is your name?"
The answer came. ANNA
Our eyes widened.
"How old are you?" Mum asked.
NINE
Just a little girl. Really?

"Where are you?"
BYTHEWINDOW.

That was enough for us. We stared at the closed curtains in silence, then put the board away.

I used to enjoy a good horror film. (The spooky rather than the gory kind.) It is fun to be scared sometimes. Less so now I know that certain situations are not the complete fantasy I once presumed them to be.

Of course, the movies are mostly over-dramatized, but a few have an uncomfortable ring of truth. In the waiting room, I am often asked what I think of certain spooky films, and if those events could really happen, so I have decided to briefly list a few.

My favourite has to be 'What Dreams May Come' with Robin Williams. Not really a scary film, I grant you, but very close to the way things could be. Our surroundings on the other side can indeed be created by the power of thought. Those higher can seek out someone lower to try to help them, but those who are lower cannot go up without first gaining understanding. Animals do have an afterlife. Soul mates do exist. All in all, I would recommend this film.

'The Exorcist' and 'The Exorcism of Emily Rose' are loosely based on true stories. The basic concept is indeed possible, although both have been sensationalized – especially The Exorcist.

It is a physical impossibility for a person's head to spin right round.

'The Entity' is also vaguely based on a true story, with Hollywood giving a huge helping hand. A dubious character in spirit could attach themselves to someone in the right circumstances, but dry-ice is not going to have any effect on the afterlife.

I enjoyed 'Poltergeist' and its sequels. All excessively larger than life, which makes them a great nightmare-free watch. I particularly like the one with Will Samson, maybe because he reminds me of someone.

There are lots of scary films about the devil – 'The Omen'; 'End of Days' etc. Although these are fantasy, I'm afraid the devil does exist. He would like us to believe he doesn't, because then we are easier to fool. He won't make you burst into flames. He will just low-key suggest you do the wrong thing and pretend the thought was yours.

'Ghost' is a good one. Lighthearted and not too scary, but with a few good points. Whoopi Goldberg going into trance and being left exhausted, although done for comedic effect, is actually not far from the truth. Someone being suddenly killed and not realising they are dead is common, and I'm afraid the nasties coming to take the baddies is pretty accurate.

As they say on Crimewatch, "Events like these are very rare. Don't have nightmares."

Mum & Dad   Mum's Mum (Grandma)

My mum with her mum, dad and brother, Tom

Childhood Days

Mum with my dad's parents.

With my dad and brothers, Alan & Paul

David with his mum and sister Annette

My David

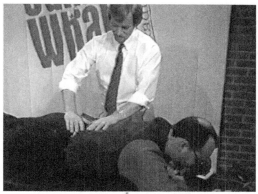

The James Whale Show

Stanley Park, Blackpool

Backstage

In Circle

The Russacks

At A Charity Function

A Super-Natural Laxative?

When people are introduced to the idea that the spirit world is all around us, it is surprising what crosses their minds.

Over the years, dozens of people have discreetly asked me if they are being watched in their most intimate moments. One young girl, after receiving messages from her mum, asked, "If she is with me all the time, what about when I'm with my boyfriend?" Her expression gave away her meaning. She looked pretty mortified at the thought, as did the pale-looking young man with her, who had fears that their relationship was about to become purely platonic.

The truth is, once they have settled into the way things work over there, your loved ones can be with you at any time. However, this does not mean they are with you *all* the time.

When those in the spirit world see that you are in personal circumstances, they step back and respect your privacy. Believe me, chances are they have no desire to be there any more than you would want them to be! It is as if they step backwards through a curtain, to another dimension, until a more appropriate moment arises.

I once mentioned to Blue Cloud, while he was speaking through David in trance, (more on this later), that people were asking me questions and I was afraid of giving them inaccurate information. I know that advising people wrongly could be of detriment to me as well as them. (We are all accountable for the decisions we make, as well as the influence we exercise over others.) There was simple wisdom in his answer. "Never be afraid to say 'I don't know.'"

With this in mind, I have checked and double-checked that those answers in this book which go beyond my personal experience, are correct. I am only able to give you the information because, at some point, I asked David - or a dead Indian.

Like a seed underground grows up toward the light then out into the open air, when we die, our souls extend into the world of spirit, to different surroundings where new rules apply.

The spirit world is not actually up in the sky, it is all around us. David makes the comparison to radio waves, which are also all around, but invisible. Each channel is on a different frequency. Turn the dial just a little, and you switch to another, but those broadcasting on the stations cannot hear each other, and as a rule, we only hear one channel a time – unless we pick up some interference and catch an indistinct glimpse into another world.

I was six years old when I paid a last visit to my paternal grandfather's cottage; a little girl in bunches and a home-sewn cotton dress, taking giant strides to bridge the same stone steps which had left a dent in my father's forehead when he was a boy.

My granddad had passed away, and we were there to make the necessary arrangements.

The living room was homely but dark and musty. It smelled of pipe tobacco and old books. The solitary window looked out onto a wall, with just a foot-worn staircase between glass and stone. The steps led to an elevated garden, barely visible through the small and yellowing, top window panes. My childish heart always raced at the thought of this forbidden lawn, which held a particular magic to me. It was rectangular, with a stunning flower border – home to a mysterious black tulip and a host of fat-bottomed spiders. I was closely guarded, despite the clamor of adult activity, and only allowed to climb the story-high stairway when firmly clutching my father's hand, in case playtime led me to plummet from the edges to the concrete below. The stuff of maternal nightmares!

There were treasures in that room, fit to entertain any lone child, adrift on a sea of adult chatter. A battered tin of buttons, long-since abandoned by the seamstress, was now played with by the granddaughter whom everyone declared she would have loved. A tawdry box containing a game called Crown & Anchor and a cribbage board, complete with spent matches, also fit the bill, but what fascinated me most was the owl.

High on the wall to the right of the door, hung a children's dream of a clock. It was a metal owl with sunken eyes of bright orange and a hooked beak. The timepiece was on its belly, and beneath the clawed feet hung pine cone weights, suspended on long chains. With every tick, the eyes moved left then right, and my mouth opened a little wider.

Noticing his daughter's enchantment, my bereaved dad hoisted me shoulder high to take a better look. I can still see my small fingers reaching for the cones and taking the cold, heavy weight in my hand as my thumb investigated every bump

The cream-coloured aga in the corner emitted the constant heat of a family's tea-brewing tradition. Here was the hearth where my newly born father had been left in the grate by a midwife who, closing the door behind her, had announced that he soon would be dead. His life had been saved by a neighbour, who wrapped him in a towel and waved him up and down in front of the fire until blue turned to pink and he took his first hearty gulp of smoke-filled, damp air.

That evening in my granddad's home, my mum was playing cards with my great-uncle, while Dad explored the bedrooms. As she sat in the living room, a voice in her head kept saying, "Look in the bottom drawer." When my dad came downstairs, she said to him, "I don't know what you are looking for, and I don't want anything, but look in the bottom drawer." He explained that he had already looked, but she told him to go back and look again.

He went into the master bedroom and emptied the bottom dresser drawer. Nothing. Then, as an afterthought, he lifted the lining paper. Underneath were the insurance papers he had been searching for. From their home in the spirit world, our loved ones can still keep an eye on us and even touch base with a helping hand, on occasion.

When people pass over, they first have to acclimatise to their new surroundings. It can be confusing, but as they learn and adjust it is an exciting time with much to come to terms with and understand. Their loved ones long passed, come to visit with them, and then their life on Earth is played back to them like a movie, and is analysed. They soon come to realise the effects that their words and actions had on the world and the people in it. As they view their unselfish actions, they may feel themselves begin to rise. Their thoughtless actions, on the other hand, will cause them to sink lower.

They will be asked why they did certain things and must take full responsibility for their actions if they are to progress. After a time of contemplation, they arrive at their destination; the place they deserve to be, where they are surrounded by like-minded people.

The spirit world does not consist of just one plane of existence. The murderer will not go to the same place as the victim.

There are many realms; many dimensions, and once we arrive at our primary destination, we continue learning, progressing, and trying to spiritually advance through these planes, striving always for heaven.

We learn and progress spiritually, and as we do, we move up through the seven dimensions or planes, until at last, we have earned our place in heaven. David talks about the individual spirit planes and what they are like, in *'The Other Side; A Psychic's Story'* and also in *'Stairway to Heaven'*.

Just as there is a heaven, there is also a hell (or the pits, as David calls it), which is similarly divided into various levels that reach down infinitely. It is the balance of things. Everything must have an opposite. How would we appreciate what is good if there was no bad? If we fail to live an unselfish lifestyle, this is where we will go. Progression is open to everyone, but earning your way out of these realms is a long and difficult process. Every time we do a selfish deed, it is as though we are given a brick that weighs us down. When we do good things we receive a balloon to help raise us up. Of course, it takes quite a few balloons to lift just one brick, and it takes many unselfish acts to counter our wrongdoings.

It is a pathway of progression which every person must travel. Animals, however, although they have a soul and live on after death in the spirit world, have a simpler existence. They do not have to try to progress. David often sees dogs or cats, and even horses with people who come to see him.

Apart from those from the spirit realms who return to visit us, there are some displaced souls who never left this world. These earthbound entities, or ghosts, are often reluctant to leave behind their material lives, their houses, and their lifestyle. Some don't even realise that they are dead.

The title of this chapter brings to mind one such character, who despite being earthbound, was quite an amiable chap.

Life doesn't stands still, and every sudden wind of change seemed to carry us to a place where David could reach a whole new catalogue of people. One such strange twist, saw us running a haunted pub in Chester city centre.

This walled city oozes history from its very stones, (just as the cellar occasionally oozed an unidentifiable, red, blood-like substance from one wall.) At the bottom of the road lay the remains of a Roman amphitheater, as well as the ruins of St John's Priory, which has a solid oak coffin built into its wall to remind the congregation of their mortality. The inscription, in old English, reads 'dust to dust.'

The pub itself is a listed, black and white Tudor building, and is famous locally for its signage. The lettering spells MARLBOROROUGH, the extra OR being attributed to the sign-writer seeing a ghost through the bedroom window and being so shaken that when he returned to his work he forgot his place.

Although the ghosts here are genuine, I rather suspect this spelling was down to spirits of a different kind.

The narrow building is deceptively large, stretching back towards the modern Marks & Spencer building and covering three floors. Plenty of room for our family, which was on the increase. Our first grandchild was born while we were there.

The traditional British pub with its oak-beamed ceiling was especially popular with international guests staying at the neighbouring Blossoms Hotel. Our selection of well-kept real ales was also popular in the city. It has since been converted into yet another modern, generic bar, which is rather a shame. I imagine the ghostly residents are not too pleased.

The Marlborough Arms was a feature of 'The Haunted Chester Tour', being known as one of the most haunted buildings in the city. It was certainly an ideal fit for our family, for whom this kind of phenomenon was a walk in the park. Here we co-habited with several spirit personalities, who were long-standing residents of the building.

It was while we were living in Chester that I noticed just how much David's legs were troubling him.

In the beginning, he would walk John to school, but within a year they were causing him so much pain that I had to take over, and he was no longer able to stand for extended periods behind the bar.

We didn't know what was causing the discomfort, and David wouldn't see a doctor. Life was extremely busy and we just pushed on.

While we were at the pub, Richard Felix of 'Most Haunted' fame, contacted David to arrange a meeting about the strange goings-on there. The interview was filmed for the 'Haunted Cheshire' DVD. Snippets, I believe, can be viewed on YouTube. *(Search David Drew Psychic Medium).*

In the cellar of the listed building, a previous landlord, shamed by money worries, had leaned across a barrel one dark night and slit his throat. Every time David went down the steps, the man would call his name in a stage whisper, but other than this he never spoke. However, a misty shape could often be seen on the CCTV, hovering around bar staff who had gone down to change a keg - and he had another disturbing habit. Always at 5.20 am, barrels would be heard rolling around down there, but those who were brave enough to investigate, found nothing disturbed.

The landlord was not the only ghostly tenant. In the bar area, by the fireplace, the spirit of a smartly dressed man wearing a black hat would periodically be seen. He used to like to tamper with the mantle clock, which chimed as it pleased and never kept time.

When our son, John was about nine years old, this man frightened him. It was a Sunday morning.

David was in bed, having worked the late-shift, and I was cleaning-up before the pub opened.

Chores done, I went next door to Marks and Spencer's to buy milk, and left John playing on the quiz machine. When I returned a few minutes later, he was pale and anxious.

He told me that he had seen a man by the fire, and at first thought a customer had somehow got into the pub, but then the figure disappeared before his eyes. I checked the CCTV. The ghost was not visible, but John's double-take and his reaction to the apparition were clear to see.

The living quarters above the pub were a hive of paranormal activity. Mostly it was audible. One, in particular, liked to shout us, mimicking the voices of other family members who were not even on the premises. Items would be moved around, or would disappear completely; children could be heard playing or crying; a watch placed on a high shelf was found to have the strap mysteriously sliced in half; that kind of thing.

One night after getting into bed, I was startled by a man's voice close to my ear. It said one word, 'Sarah'. I wondered if this was a case of mistaken identity, and perhaps it was, but our daughter, who was pregnant at the time, announced soon afterwards that she was going to name her baby girl, Sarah. A ghostly suggestion? A premonition? I'm not sure, but certainly something more than a coincidence.

One good thing about living in England was that when we became grandparents, our granddaughter called me Nain (which is Welsh for grandmother). No-one there knew what it meant, allowing me to retain the illusion of youth – at least until we returned to Wales.

Now, at last, I come to my point. In the gent's toilet, (which we later discovered was situated where the stables of the neighboring hotel used to stand), was a resident spirit who introduced himself to David soon after we moved in. After closing time, when there were no customers around, he would chat to David while he had a wee. (Too much information?) The gentleman's name was Gilbert, and he had been a stable-hand at the Blossoms Hotel. A convivial character with deep-set eyes, he was balding, and usually wore a herringbone jacket. He is the exception to the rule. He *did* hang about in the gents - although I'm unsure if he still saw it as the stables it once was. I often think he must miss his evening chats with David now we have gone, and I wonder if he is leading the new landlord a dance.

Your loved ones in the spirit world, have their own plans; their own things to do. There are magnificent halls of learning, where people only have to pass through to absorb knowledge. There are loved ones long passed, with whom they want to spend time

It is an exciting place, and while they will be eager to come to see you from time to time, unlike Gilbert, they certainly have more interesting fish to fry than watching you on the toilet.

Does He Tell Your Future?

An Unforeseen Circumstance

Tell me my future? He doesn't tell me ANYTHING! David once went to the auction of a hotel in Llandudno. A murder had been committed there, and he was curious to see if it would sell. When he came home, I asked him who bought it, and he announced, "We did!" I had a few choice words to impart, not due to the murder, but because I loathe cooking and had absolutely no desire to be a hotelier.

In the end, as usual, my infuriating husband won me around, and Blue Cloud Lodge, as we renamed it, (in honour of the big guy), became a spiritual retreat. To be fair, it was the ideal place for David to host psychic weekends and evenings of clairvoyance.

There is more about what was dubbed the 'murder house' in *The Other Side; A Psychic's story*. I won't dwell on the details now, but suffice to say, it was a tragic story that left several dead and injured, and three children sadly orphaned. It marked a very dark day in the history of Llandudno. The hotel had been boarded up since the incident, and neighbours would cross the road to avoid walking close by.

We resolved to bring light to the hotel again. Buildings and objects can absorb atmospheres, and this was a chilling place before we took over.

In life, we are influenced or we influence. Others could have been affected by the dark mark events had left here, but it didn't take long for David and his high-spirit friends to shine their influence into every corner. Soon it was a happy home for us, and the perfect venue for David to work.

Those who see David for a psychic reading may notice that he never uses any visual aids or props. It is his view that truly psychic people don't need them and that people who buy a book on how to read tarot cards then set themselves up as psychic, are misleading people.

Great responsibility comes with these gifts. Words affect lives, and this is something David takes very seriously. He rejects the use of tarot cards, crystal balls, bumps on the head, or tea-leaves! (This said, he did have an auntie who insisted on thrusting her china cup into his hand when he was a young boy. She couldn't grasp that he didn't need tea-leaves to tell her things, so he would hold the cup to humour her, as spirit told him what to say.)

David's primary resource when giving a reading, is the information he receives by seeing and hearing people in the spirit world. That is to say, the sitter's friends, relatives, helpers, and guide, as well as David's own guide.

This may come in the form of a message for you, some advice on your future, or simply comfort from the proof that someone you love is living on. His second source of information is drawn from the interpretation of signs and pictures which spirit show him within your aura. In his youth, he deciphered what the symbols meant. They range from the straightforward (e.g. a house which moves meaning a house-move) to the more cryptic, (e.g. a tree branching in two directions representing a parting, which may be a breakup or perhaps a death.) We will look at auras in greater depth later on. During the reading, he scribbles down the symbols he sees, as they often come and go quickly. After the reading, the sitter may, if they wish, take this paper away with them.

The direction of our lives is not pre-planned. There are certain lessons we are intended to learn, certain things it would be beneficial for us to experience, but nothing is set in stone. We will be steered towards opportunities, and tests will be laid so that we can demonstrate our worth, but we rise or fall by our own decisions.

It is not just psychics who must be careful what they say. Any time we advise someone, we run the risk of shouldering some of the blame for their actions; specifically if they take notice of us and do what turns out to be the wrong thing.

If your best friend comes to you with her marriage problems, then you tell her to stay and work things out with her husband, and she takes your advice but misses out on the path she was intended to take, you will have to answer for that when you pass over. She will answer for her actions, and you will answer for the part you played.

We have all been given the gift of free-will, and it is up to us what direction we take. If you must give an opinion, be sure to stress that you could be wrong, and tell the person that they need to decide for themselves.

We must captain our own ship; choose for ourselves between left and right; dark and light; right and wrong. If we went through this life like robots, with our actions pre-programmed, what credit would we have for our positive efforts, and how could we be held responsible for our mistakes? God hopes we will choose to do His will, and ultimately reap the rewards. Our spirit-guides try to steer us the right way. The devil is routing on the side of a darker path. Ultimately the choice is ours.

From where they are, those in spirit can see the pathway we are travelling at any given time. If there are obstacles or opportunities ahead, they can advise us accordingly. David can tell you what spirit have to say, but we all have the ability to change direction at any time. Nothing is fixed.

When I first met David, he advised me regarding the pathway I was on. He could see I was at a crossroads. I could go back to my old life if I wanted to, or move on to a new relationship (which neither of us knew was to be with him.)

Once David and I entered into a relationship, the dynamic changed. Any potential to give me advice on my future evaporated. The reason is a simple one. I have mentioned that psychic ability is intended to help others. When my life became indistinct from his, my future became his future. Any advance warning on my forthcoming situation would have been an insight into his, and it isn't meant to work that way.

Although he knew full well that his abilities were not to be used to benefit himself, David couldn't resist putting this theory to the test one time. We were newly married and still living in Blackpool. Money was tight and bills were flooding into our new home faster than income. Just like the Grinch, David had a wonderful, awful idea! He would go to the casino with what money we had and win enough to pay all the bills. He would go on the roulette-wheel and predict the numbers. What could possibly go wrong?

I stared at him in disbelief. Although we had been together for little over a year, I understood enough to realise this was never going to work. "They won't let you win," I told him.

"But I can do this easily!" He protested.
"Yes, in theory," I told him, "but they won't LET you win. Not like this."

He thought for a moment. "Maybe not - but it's worth a try."
He put on his dinner suit and prepared to head off to the Vegas of the north. I watched him from my

armchair, tutting under my breath.

I was in bed when he came home, penniless and full of explanations. Every time he bet on a number, it came up - not when he had money on it – but the time after. The numbers chased him around the table, letting him know that yes, he could predict the numbers, but he wasn't going to profit from it.

Refraining from saying, "I told you so," I rolled my eyes and went back to sleep.

Although David can predict nothing of his own future, I would like to share with you an interesting story about one occasion when the spirit world couldn't resist dropping a cheeky hint.

It was 31st October 1995, and David was holding an evening of clairvoyance. The venue had decked the room out with candles, pumpkins, and the like. David doesn't usually buy into the commercial side of Halloween, which is the night before All Souls Day, a time when the church remembers the dead, but as it was for charity and the cause was a good one, he agreed to go ahead.

The evening was a phenomenal success, but at the end of the night, David found himself frustrated by a particular message. As he took the stage at the beginning of the evening, he announced, "There are three people in this room who are expecting a baby. One lady already knows, but the other two don't – despite the fact the damage has already been done."

This prompted a nervous giggle to surf around the room. "I don't know who you are yet, but I will find you before the night is out."

The first pregnancy was identified early on, after passing on just a couple of messages. The young woman blushed and confirmed that she was nine weeks pregnant. He refused to reveal the gender, before advising her to start knitting in blue!

The second woman seemed shocked, although the elbow-dig from her friend indicated it was not a complete surprise.

The third announcement never came. This was the source of David's vexation. He had been determined to find all three.

"Why would I be told there were three pregnancies, but only shown the identity of two?" He was puzzled.
It had never happened before.
We didn't guess it, but there was a reason for this absence of detail.

Two weeks later the mystery was solved.

That Halloween night, I had harbored no suspicion that it could possibly be me. We were soon to embark on David's next international tour, which was to involve a lot of flying and a heavy schedule.
Three days before we left, I realised the need to take a test, just to reassure myself that there was no chance I might be pregnant.

I kept this to myself. After all, it was very unlikely.

The result was a shock. My head was spinning. Mum, who was staying with us, was waiting for me to get ready. It was her birthday and we were going out for cake and coffee. David had to be the first to know, but he was out. The test was all I could think about, but I had to keep quiet.

Life was so busy. David was overworked, Blue Cloud Lodge was buzzing, and we already had two girls. I didn't know how David would feel about it. I didn't know how *I* felt about it!

I waited for David to come home, and met him at the car, climbing into the passenger seat.
"What?"
"I was just thinking," I made a start, "how would you feel if I was pregnant?"
"Why?" He was dismissive.
"Because I've taken a test – and I am."
He looked stunned.
"I don't know how we are going to cope," I continued, "and I need some time to get used to this."
"We'll be fine! But are you sure?"
"Yes, but please don't tell anyone until I've got my head around it."
"Ok." He said, and opened the car door. My mum was approaching the gate. "Mary," he shouted excitedly, "Jane's pregnant." And burst into tears. Nine months later, David was cutting the cord, and our son, John became the newest member of the Drew tribe.

Throughout our marriage, other than predictions on my future, certain of David's remarkable and infuriating gifts endure. He often knows when I have met an old friend while out shopping - and trying to sneak that new handbag in under the radar is a dangerous game.

"Why would you want to hide it from me?" He would seem hurt. "Did you think I would mind you buying it?"

A girl just likes to keep her little secrets sometimes. Right? This psychic ability has been known to sap all the fun out of secret shopping, and especially gift buying! I can't remember a year when David didn't end up having his birthday present early!

Our girls will tell you that having a psychic dad is not all giggles. Every father thinks there is no boy good enough for their daughter. Add to this the ability to list the misdemeanors of boyfriends he has never met, and the prospect of a normal teenage relationship is dead in a ditch.

When it comes to loved ones who have passed away, it is a different story. He can and does give me messages from time to time.

On many occasions he has seen my mum and dad, both of whom he loved dearly, as well as my uncle, my grandmother and various other relatives, who he never met in life.

One winter afternoon he had a vision of a family friend, whom we had not seen for some months.

She was shown to be lying in a coffin. It prompted me to phone her nursing-home, and discover, with some sadness, that she had recently passed. Despite the warning, I was strangely shocked to hear it confirmed. I suppose I was hoping that, for once, he had made a mistake.

David's premonitions provoke mixed reactions from the family, and don't seem to follow any pattern. He could tell his mum when long lost relatives were going to visit, but had no prior warning when he found himself in the midst of the Birmingham pub bombings.

We were having a family holiday in Scotland at The Russacks Hotel, St Andrews when David had the worst premonition imaginable. The kind of vision you pray you'll never see.

It was December 1988. The hotel was beautifully dressed, ready for a traditional Scottish Christmas. The girls were still small, and wide eyes and mouths told of their enchantment at the enormous Christmas tree and opulent décor, which was like a set from an old festive movie.

The weather was bleak and the coastline merciless, which made the cracks and pops of the logs on the hotel's open fires, all the more inviting. David's work schedule had been full-on for some time, and despite the excruciatingly long journey to reach The Russacks, in the end we were glad to have made the effort.

It was a treat to have time to relax with the children and each other. Two days later, however, the mood was unexpectedly sullied.

It was early evening and we were seated at the dinner table. I was chatting inanely as we waited for our meal, and looked up, mid-sentence, to see that David's expression had changed. The calm, relaxed demeanor was gone, his complexion was grey and his eyes, suddenly lifeless, stared at something behind me. I turned, but there was no-one there.

"David?" No response, "What's wrong?"
The waitress brought our evening meal, which seemed to bring him back to this world, but he looked through the table as if there was nothing there.

When the waitress left, he spoke.
"I just saw a plane crash. There was a ball of fire and the nose broke off - then it just fell into pieces and dropped out of the sky."

I was speechless. His words caught me off-guard. I wanted to say something that would comfort him. I could suggest it was just his imagination, but we both knew it was more than that.

You can leave the ringing phone behind you when you need a break, but there was no escape from a gift – or maybe a curse – like this.
"What can we do? Can we warn someone?" It was a futile question.

"Who?" he answered, playing with his knife. "I don't know when it will be; or where." Then he looked at me with helpless resignation. "It could be anywhere. I can't stop this."

I searched for an answer, nausea overwhelming me when it didn't come.

"Then you need to put it out of your mind. It could be years from now, and maybe something will change. Something that will prevent it." It was a pathetic attempt to take some weight from his shoulders, but I had to say something.

He didn't sleep much that night. We woke from our restlessness, determined to put the omen behind us, not least for the sake of the girls. I struck up a cheerful demeanor and resolved to make this a happy day.

After breakfast, it was decided we would wrap up against the cold and walk the ruins of the abbey. By the time we strolled back into the square, all portents of doom were forgotten and we were ready to warm up with a hot chocolate and a snifter.

Sunset saw the world put to rights, and soon we were dressing for the evening meal, after a hot bubble bath. David was in the bathroom when Ayesha clicked the TV on. I caught my breath. There were images of aircraft debris. The ticker tape across the bottom read, 'Lockerbie, Scotland'. I turned up the sound.
"David! Quick!"

He looked absolutely defeated. Two-hundred and seventy people had been killed, when PAN-AM flight 103 from Frankfurt to Detroit was blown up as it flew over the ill-fated Scottish town.

Two days later, we drove home, silently passing the wounded Lockerbie and the crater which now replaced its North-bound carriageway.

Omens or premonitions of this kind are thankfully rare to the likes of you and me. For David they are all too common, although few are as shocking as the Lockerbie disaster. We can all be receptive to signs and sensations to some extent. Having spoken with many on this subject, it seems a common theme to know who is on the telephone before we pick up, or have someone on your mind, only to find they are in trouble or suddenly make contact with you.

More ambiguous signs can come in the form of feathers, butterflies, robins and rainbows, whose veracity is hit and miss.

I remember a stressful time, when our house-move had fallen through, and we were feeling particularly unsettled. It was just after daybreak.

I was having trouble sleeping and went downstairs to get a drink. As I climbed back up the stairs, I was drawn to the full spectrum of coloured light which was emanating from the bathroom.

The tiled walls were lit up in reds, blues and yellows.

I had never seen anything like it. I went to the window, and saw a rainbow, which appeared to be just a few streets away. I couldn't understand why it would be shining in our house. I quickly retrieved my phone and took a photograph to show David. It seemed like a deliberate sign – perhaps everything would be okay

Sure enough, a few weeks later we found our next house. It was perfect. Then I realised that the end of the rainbow had been pointing right to it. A framed copy of that photo now hangs in our home; a little picture to remind us of the bigger picture.

Throughout life, we can be influenced by our surroundings, which can affect our mood for better or worse – or we can create our own impressions and change the environment.

A few years ago we visited Poland. While we were there we made the essential visit to Auschwitz, taking the trip by car from central Krakow, where we were staying. I was nervous. Knowing that I could be over-sensitive at times, I imagined I might be overwhelmed by the mark left by all that suffering. When we had been in Israel, visiting a holocaust museum, we saw the children's drawings, the piles of shoes and heard the heartbreaking stories. I had to make use of the emergency exit halfway round. I waited outside to compose myself, taking in the smell of the trees and the view across Jerusalem to clear my head. This promised to be worse.

When we passed through the famous iron gateway at Oswiecim, into the concentration camp, I was surprised by the atmosphere. Far from feeling the desperation of the inmates, the hopelessness of their plight, all I sensed was a terrible evil.

Nothing was growing there. There were no birds. The silent site was an abyss, as though the people who had been held there were gone forever, but a stain from the dark souls who once enslaved them still remained.

When we went home, people asked if we enjoyed the trip. You could never describe it as enjoyable, but we were glad we went. I feel that everyone who has the opportunity to go should take it. David wasn't able to visit every area, as he couldn't walk more than a few yards. We took the trip just in time. His mobility was rapidly declining.

We can all be sensitive to our surroundings, and the workings of spirit. Just keep an open mind, and remember, all things for a reason. There are very few coincidences.

My father shared his birthday with David; the eighteenth of December - exactly one week before Christmas Day. The two were good pals and occasional drinking buddies. To my amazement, David was old fashioned enough to ask him for my hand in marriage, after which the two shared a bottle of whisky, and a few choice stories about me, either in celebration or commiseration. I'm not sure which.

Shortly before my dad died, David told him, as they passed the bottle, that he loved and respected him; sentiments that men don't usually voice. He often remarks that he is so pleased that he did this. Perhaps I should have seen it as a portent of things to come.

In the months following this boozy conversation, my father was diagnosed with an abdominal aortic aneurism after noticing a strange pulse in his belly. He was faced with two major operations. The first was to repair his heart so he would be able to withstand the second, which was to fix the aneurism.

As they wheeled him to theatre, the surgeon stopped the gurney to point out that the procedure was very high risk, to which my dad smiled and answered, "It's okay. I've got friends in high places."
The surgeon, somewhat taken aback, added, "I'm not joking!"
To which my dad replied, "Neither am I."
He had faith enough to know that, whatever happened, he would be looked after.

I was worried during that first operation, but David wasn't fazed. He reassured me that Dad would be fine, and true to his prediction, he was. The second operation, a few months later, was a different story.

On the morning of the surgery, I was hoovering to keep myself busy, when a series of phrases kept repeating in my head. "What do you want to keep him here for? Better things are waiting for him. Why keep him here? He deserves better."

I didn't want to hear this and kept trying to dismiss the thoughts as imagination, mentally swatting at the words like troublesome mosquitos.

Keep busy.

Say a prayer.

Passing David's office, I caught sight of him seated at his desk, obviously disturbed and distracted. Now I was worried! I could tell something was wrong this time.

Within the hour he was pacing around the house, seemingly in a world of his own. He didn't volunteer what was wrong, and I was too afraid to ask.

That afternoon I phoned the hospital and was informed that the operation had gone well and my dad was in recovery. I was so relieved, but David's mood didn't lift. Then, out of the blue, he suggested we go to the cinema. This was unusual. Normally I would have to drag him there. I could tell he was trying to distract me.

We sat through the early evening showing of 'Titanic', only half watching. When the film finished, David was still subdued, and immediately phoned home. After the call, he took my hand and we walked home in silence. I hadn't heard the conversation and he didn't say anything, but I knew my dad, who I had spoken to that morning, was dead.

In the months that followed, David explained that my father had been given a choice.

He had been shown the place he would go and asked if he wanted to stay or go back to his old life. His children were grown and settled, and he had been in great pain. He always said that dying was just a natural part of life, which everyone must do eventually. Uncomfortable but necessary – much like being born. It seems he simply decided to gracefully accept his promotion.

David saw my dad soon after he passed. He was standing behind the bar in Blue Cloud Lodge, our spiritual retreat. After that, the whisky (his alcohol of choice), always dripped from the optic. No matter how many times we replaced the fitting or swapped it for a different spirit, it was always only the whisky.

My mother was also fond of David. Strange perhaps for son and mother-in-law to have a kind of mutual admiration society. He would often throw out a good-humoured mother-in-law joke from the stage when she was around. They had an easy rapport, and in later years when I would shop for her, she wouldn't rest unless I brought some treat back for 'our David.'

The final weeks in hospital were hard on her. At eighty-nine, her body was shutting down. Each day she would say, "If I could just see David, I know everything would be alright."

When he visited, her face lit up. She held his hand so tightly, and for days afterwards, she talked about his visit with a sparkle in her eyes.

She passed peacefully in hospital a few days later, and she was, indeed, alright.

Since her passing, which is recent at the time of writing, David has seen her in our house several times, and she has also appeared to our daughter, Ayesha, who, being old enough to sit in the regular psychic development circle which David held, often experiences random spirit contact. My brother has also felt her presence. As for me, I woke and briefly saw her sitting at the foot of the sofa I was lying on, and I have felt her firmly poke me in the back once or twice, as was her habit.

It seems Mum is happy, but still a little bemused by her surroundings and the workings of her exciting new world.

One might imagine, with all David's knowledge of life being eternal and death being as simple as walking into another room, that he would be the most composed person at a funeral. This is far from the truth. He is probably the most emotional person I have ever met. He knows that the deceased is fine, but misses their presence and empathises with those left behind.

Due to his experience of public speaking and knowledge of the afterlife, he is often asked to speak at funerals. He hates it! Without exception, he *always* breaks down in tears. His obvious affection for the deceased does him credit, and if anything, only adds to the occasion, but he is terribly embarrassed.

It is the physical presence of our loved ones that we mourn. We miss them beside us. If they had emigrated to Australia, we would be sad to see them go. The fact that they are safe and happy somewhere else, does not mitigate our selfish sense of loss, or sadness at what they might have suffered before they passed.

At age twenty-four, David lost his own mother to a brain tumor. She was only fifty-eight.

Joan Drew had suffered from chronic headaches for years. Eventually, the doctor decided to send her into hospital for some tests. When David and Tim went to visit her, the doctor met them as they entered the ward, taking the young men to one side.

Her x-rays were illuminated as he explained that there was a tumour, and to remove the cancer he would need to take away part of her brain, which would likely leave her with a severe loss of cognitive ability.

They were in shock. There had been no clue that it was anything so serious, and now they were standing in an office, being asked for a decision. Should they operate?

Tim, despite being the elder of the two, looked to David for the answer.
"Let her go."
Tim nodded in agreement, trusting his little brother's judgement.

She was discharged from hospital then cared for at home by their sister Annette until she passed away. The end came sooner than predicted, but it was a blessing. Nature has a way of preparing us for death. As illness takes hold, life becomes less attractive to us, and the prospect of an end to our earthly labours is often welcomed.

When the day of the funeral came, David was inconsolable. The extent of his grief took the family by surprise. They expected him to take it in his stride and overlooked the fact that, despite all his knowledge of the spirit world, the young man, quite naturally, missed his mum.

Only once, since her passing, has David seen his mother, although I am sure she is often around. You may have read the details in *The Other Side; A Psychic's Story.*

It was soon after she passed. She seemed to blow in through a closed window, billowing the curtains wildly. She told him to tell the family she was happy, before disappearing into the stillness for the last time.

It would be nice if he could see her whenever he wanted, but this is not how it is meant to be. Neither can he predict natural disasters, if they are to affect him directly.

In June 1993 the floods came to Llandudno.

Heavy rain and thunderstorms saw most of the town, including Blue Cloud Lodge, submerged. In the midst of the mayhem, David had a heart attack. He was only thirty-nine.

He arrived home to find three feet of water inside the hotel, and almost instantly collapsed, leaving me holding his head and shoulders above water until the ambulance arrived.

His health has been a constant worry to me for many years. I know he has no fear of death, but I do wish he wouldn't keep me on my toes! I already live in dread of the day I have to lose him to better things.

By ten o'clock that evening, I was standing, barefoot and soaking wet, (I had injured my foot, which had swollen out of my shoe,) outside Llandudno General Hospital, having settled David onto a ward for the night. I had no idea how I was going to get home.

In the early hours, a nurse coming on shift recognised who David was. He was wide awake when she came to check on him. Routine completed, she leaned over and spoke to him on a personal level.
"Can you see anything with me?"

Feeling better and desperate for a smoke, he saw an opportunity to barter.
"I'll tell you what I am seeing, if you take me somewhere I can have a cigarette."

Soon he was surrounded by a group of excited nurses who had hatched a plan. They wheeled the bed with him in it, into the laundry room, and opened the window to let the smoke out. Both parties were more than happy with the trade.

Within a week he was home. The local press took pictures of him lying in bed, bare-chested. He was well enough by then to joke that the article could go on page three, adding a request that they advertise the fact that his next evening of clairvoyance was cancelled – due to unforeseen circumstances.

We each settle into our daily routine; our jobs; our relationships, and it is easy to presume that life will always be the same. When boredom sets in, remember that one day your reality will shift. In this life or the next, everything will change. As Heraclitus famously mused, 'Change is the only constant.' The transformation may come in the shape of a loss; your job; a parent; a spouse; even your life, or it may present as an opportunity; meeting your soulmate; a career move; a new baby perhaps. Everything changes. Only God remains the same. The one constant in all our little stories. The arm to lean on in the dark.

I find it unsettling that nothing stays the same. When the wind of change blows, I turn to my favourite Old Testament quote, Isiah 40:8; 'The grass withers and the flowers fall, but the word of our God endures forever.'

This helps me ride the wave.

Every story must, in its timely fashion, move on to a new scene. This is how we learn and experience different things. The forward motion is perpetual. Even death is only a change of destination.

One little-known, but major transformation, which eventually comes to us all, came early for David, but as we know, his personal circumstance tends to be a little unorthodox.

Most of us don't know why we are here. It might be to learn and experience something specific, to teach, or to make a difference in some other way. David was given his gifts, and the ability to remember what the spirit world is like, so that he could help people to understand that there is life after death, and that how you live this life is of the utmost importance. It will determine what kind of place you go to. It's an age-old, but long-forgotten concept, and it needed driving home. The 'eat, drink and be merry' mentality was committing too many to misery after they passed over. Someone had to do something, and David got the job.

During the early part of his life, he was largely oblivious to this. He knew he was different and was puzzled as to why he saw dead people – or more to the point, why others didn't, but he began this life (as do we all), with a blank page.

Unlike the rest of us, his intended purpose required that, when the time was right, he should remember his existence before he came into this world.

He needed to access that information. If you try to place yourself in his shoes, you will perhaps begin to appreciate a little of how difficult this was for him.

When we are in the realms of spirit, there comes a time when we begin to remember our previous earthly lives, and the time between them spent on the other side. By this time, we are not limited by the constraints of an earthly brain, and our spiritual understanding is such that we can cope with the enormity of this realisation, and the transformation we undergo, as all our previous personalities and knowledge, merge into one. We become an accumulation of everyone we have ever been.

A little difficult to digest? Of course! An infant at school cannot digest a university lecture. Our earthly brain has limits and is not advanced enough to fully understand. When I was seven, I asked my dad how much money he had in the bank. I have never forgotten his answer. "It doesn't matter if you don't know." There is wisdom in this. There are a million questions to ask about the world to come, but it's futile to rush. Mild winters bring the buds too soon, only to see them perish in the February frosts. Let lessons come slowly; one at a time. The first needs to be truly understood before the next will make any sense. When the time is right, it will all lay down before us like a completed jigsaw.

For David, the transition of becoming the accumulation needed to happen while he was on earth It began slowly, with a drip-feed, and culminated in a massive spiritual download.

Initially, he kicked against the process. He just wanted to lead a normal life; to be the same as everyone else. Those who have read, *The Other Side; A Psychic's Story* will be familiar with David's experience of this.

This is mine.

My darling husband had not been his jocular self for a few days. He was clearly stressed, and reluctant to articulate the reason why. As we watched Coronation Street, I could see his mind was elsewhere, his chin in hand, his eyes serious; focused on something high up to the right of the fireplace. I pretended not to notice. He stood up sharply, and strode off toward the kitchen, returning a few minutes later with a cup of tea.

I recognised the signs. He was annoyed. But not with me, so perhaps I shouldn't pry. When the program finished, I walked behind his chair and put my arms around his neck, resting my chin on his shoulder.
"Are you okay? Is there anything I can do?"
He was agitated. Evasive.
"I'm fine." And he gave me an affectionate but dismissive pat on the hand.

So it was for a few weeks. David was distracted. At times he seemed upset. Afraid even.

If we took the girls to the park or went shopping in town, he was his old self for a short while, then the dark cloud would descend as his worried look returned.

Each day the pressure mounted, and David became increasingly distressed. One evening, as I moved to embrace him, I saw tears in those blue eyes I loved so much. Those eyes which concealed a vault of secrets.

"I have to go away for a little while. Just to get my head together." A slight hesitation. "When I come home will you still love me? I need you."
"Of course I will." I took his face in my hands. "I will *always* love you."
His strange reply came from far away.
"But I don't even know if I will *like myself!*"

That afternoon he threw a few things into an overnight bag, then kissed me like it was goodbye.

The following few days were calm, but not peaceful. I trusted that everything would be alright, accepted that there were certain things which it didn't matter if I couldn't understand. I prayed for him, went about my days, and remembered to breathe in and out until he came home.

Days passed slowly until I heard a key turn in the door. There he was, eyes shining; a clear and deeper blue than I remembered. He lifted me in his arms, kissing me hello.

The love felt the same, the touch was the same, but *something* had changed.

I leaned back and searched his face. He caught my puzzled gaze.

"What?" The voice was mellow; serious; too stoic.

This was someone else, but not a stranger. Smiling, I asked the question.

"Where is the man I married?"

There was a pause.

"He's still in here." A gentle smile, and a look so intense I had to lower my eyes. "I wouldn't leave you."

Peculiar days followed. David had the same uncanny air of serenity about him. He would notice me staring, and immediately tell a joke or recite some familiar phrase in an unfamiliar tone. I was not consoled. It was weird! The intonation and expression didn't fit. My alarmed face must have been a picture.

He practiced as the days passed, and pretty soon I had a version of my husband I could recognise. He slipped into new, old habits, and life moved forward again, inch by inch, one heartbeat at a time.

He was still David, but there was something more. I can equate it to meeting up with an old school friend after thirty years have passed.

A friend who has lived through experiences you didn't share; life-lessons that changed him; who has gained wisdom, but essentially, is the same person.

So David was home, and no longer anxious about his peculiar mission. The confusion had passed. He needn't have worried about losing his identity. It could be said he was more himself than he had ever been.

What is a Trance Medium?

Is there anybody there?

There are many spiritualist mediums on the psychic circuit, some of whom are very good. However, very few are 'complete' mediums, so to speak, and hardly any are trance mediums.

'Complete medium' is a term often used to identify someone who has the full range of psychic gifts, i.e. clairvoyance, clairaudience, clairsentience, healing, psychometry, and trance-mediumship. Most have only one or two of these, but range of ability does not necessarily equate to quality of the same. A genuine, experienced medium with just one of these gifts is all you need.

When press articles refer to David's gifts, they often include trance-mediumship in the list. As a result, I am often asked what this means. The answer, though interesting, has been known to unnerve people.

Sit comfortably, dim the lights, and let us delve into the mysterious world of the séance!

There have been some famous hoaxes in the history of Spiritualism, but the truth behind the genuine, sequestered séance, unveils a meditative and refreshing experiment into the merging of worlds.

The word 'séance' may well evoke visions of horror films and spinning heads, however, the word simply means 'sitting', and when conducted correctly, the practice is quite safe. David prefers to use the term 'circle', as it is not nearly so melodramatic.

To sit in circle, or séance, is to conduct a psychic experiment, and it should never be undertaken unless headed by an experienced medium who can take control of any situation which might arise. It is essential that someone present can identify who, in spirit, they are dealing with and what is taking place.

The process is simple. A group of like-minded people sit in a circle, in a room with subdued lighting. Candlelight works best, and soft music is often played to encourage complete relaxation. This helps sitters be more receptive to spiritual influences. For this reason, circles are usually held in the evening, as the atmosphere tends to be more peaceful. There is no need for a table or indeed to hold hands, but once the session begins, it is essential that no one leaves, or breaks the circle.

As the group sit, a ring of spirit guides and helpers gather behind them. This forms a protective outer circle in the spirit world and acts as a barrier to shield them from any lower spirit entity which may want to draw close. Breaking the circle would compromise this protection and disrupt the flow of psychic energy, which is pooled by the participants, and naturally flows from person to person.

This energy is utilized by those in the spirit world, as they try to communicate in a variety of ways.

Without exception, David opens every circle with a prayer. This helps protect those involved, and elevates everyone's thoughts to a more spiritual level. Prayers may also be offered for anyone needing healing or comfort, as well as for those in the spirit world who may be confused, or in need of help.

As people sit in quiet meditation, they begin to experience various sights, sounds, and sensations, which they are encouraged to share with the group. Temperature change is a common starting point. Some may feel burning hot while others feel a cold wind around their feet. Other preliminary experiences include being lightly touched, seeing orbs of light or even silhouettes and faces of spirit visitors who are hoping to participate in the experiment of joining two worlds. Those who sit regularly will find they are able to progressively see, hear, and feel more and more as they begin to psychically develop.

In practice, there is nothing to fear from sitting in a well- run psychic circle, although once, our cat, who had been hiding in the dark, jumped on someone's knee mid-circle and nearly gave them a heart attack!

Each psychic circle shines a bright, beam of light throughout the spirit worlds, so that not only your spirit helpers and loved ones but other souls may be attracted to it, in particular those who may be lost, confused, or in a dark place.

To them, it is like wandering in the night and seeing a house with a lamp in the window. They make towards it hoping for rescue, and there they receive the help they need. Some specifically named 'rescue circles', sit especially for this purpose.

Now, groundwork completed, we come to trance-mediumship. When a trance-medium, such as David, sits in circle, then spirit may choose to use the psychic energy available either to change his facial features (called transfiguration) or occupy his body to communicate directly with the sitters. If you have seen the film 'Ghost' with Whoopi Goldberg, there is a rather comedic representation of this procedure, but dramatics aside, the principle is loosely the same.

To accomplish this seamlessly, practice is required, both by the host medium and the spirit visitor. The medium must learn to trust his guide, and relinquish consciousness, not unlike allowing yourself to fall backward, trusting that your colleague will catch you.

Blue Cloud, as David's spirit guide, acts as his door-keeper. That is to say, it is his responsibility to keep him safe and allow or deny access to whoever is hoping to speak through his body. In this state, David is at his most vulnerable, and having someone he can trust at the helm is essential.

I usually sit to David's right, and try to direct the flow of psychic energy toward him. A fair amount of energy is required for communication to be successful.

Having an experienced sitter close to the medium can be reassuring. I ensure that no-one acts in a manner that could be detrimental to him, and also, being accustomed to the timbre of Blue Cloud's voice, I am usually able, when necessary, to interpret what he is saying for the other sitters.

As BC grants access to the spirit who wishes to speak, David's spirit leaves his body and is suspended safely, in a sleep-like state as the newcomer enters.

Blue Cloud once explained the process to me, like this.

"In hospital, you have the life-supporting machine. A man is on this machine, his spirit is out. Sometimes they say, 'Do we turn the machine off?' If the spirit has gone and the silver cord is broken, they might as well.

When we come through, it is as if we keep the body on the life-supporting machine. The spirit is held in a trance state. When we leave, a second or two later, his spirit returns."

Those who have read David's books will understand that our spirit is connected to the body by a silver cord. When we sleep, our spirit (or real self) can leave the physical body and travel through this world and the next, still attached via this cord. This is widely known as astral travel or astral projection.

Only when the cord breaks does death occur, as the

spirit is unable to return to its earthly counterpart, which is left as an empty shell.

Near-death experiences occur when the spirit is out of the body, perhaps observing their surroundings, but the cord is intact. Once the silver cord breaks, there is no going back.

Astral travel is usually involuntary and can take place in this world or the next. You can travel ahead in sleep state, and visit a town in advance of your actual trip. This can cause a place to seem familiar to you – a sense of deja-vu. You can visit a friend or loved one, and they may see you in their dream, or if they are awake, maybe think you a ghost. You probably won't remember everything, but often some remnant remains.

It is also possible to travel through the veil and visit the spirit realms, perhaps meeting a departed loved one. Usually, you have no control over this, although I do remember a time when David intentionally took me with him to visit Blue Cloud. It had been a while since I had spoken with him through David, and I missed my friend. Snuggled up in bed one night, I whispered over David's shoulder.

"It seems like ages since I spoke to BC."
I hoped that perhaps he would suggest holding a circle. His sleepy response took me by surprise.
"I'll take you to see him."

As I held him close, his words dissolved and all

consciousness was gradually cast aside.

A blanket of darkness with flecks of coloured light rushed past me on all sides, as I rode pillion on what seemed almost like some kind of magic carpet. Strange landscapes swirled below as we dipped and turned, and I held on tight, exhilarated by the ride but confident I was safe. Shadowy mountains were beneath us, when I noticed a small glow ahead. A campfire. As we drew close, I could make out a white, displaced structure, like a roofless building, which looked like a maze from above, and there before it, a figure crouched over the flames. It was Blue Cloud.

We landed beside him and David stood back. I could hardly believe I was standing next to my friend, having crossed dimensions to find him. He stared into the flames, as if in meditation, as I waited silently for his reaction. In time he raised his gaze and momentarily looked straight at me. Then he spoke three words before returning to his pose.
"Who are you?"

David thought this was hilarious! He was still laughing about it the next morning. He had taken me all that way, just to be put in my place. It was fair enough. I had ideas above my station. If he had wanted to talk, I'm sure he would have come to me.

David told me that the first time he went into deep trance, he was around fifteen years old, and it took him completely by surprise.

He had been invited to sit in a weekly circle held at the home of the president of his local spiritualist church. This particular evening, he was feeling tired after a busy day, but decided to attend nonetheless. Mrs. Woolley, a medium herself, lived in a smart but modest terraced house with eclectic furnishings and a homely atmosphere.

When David arrived, he chatted with the usual familiar faces over a cup of tea, and when everyone was there, the candle was lit and the group took their places.

As the lights were dimmed, he relaxed under the protection of the circle, and soon found himself struggling to keep his eyes open. Suddenly, his chin hit his chest and he woke with a start. All the sitters were staring at him.

Flushed with embarrassment, he began to apologise, but quickly learned he had not simply nodded off as he presumed. For twenty minutes, the spirit of a little girl called Rose had been occupying his body, while his own spirit was safely held in a hypnotic state. She had entertained the sitters with her endearing giggles as she squirmed about on the chair.

She became a frequent visitor to the circle, and it transpired that in life she had spina bifida. The more often she came through, the better her control of his body and vocal cords became, and in turn, he gained experience in controlling when, and indeed if, she made use of his body.

The first time I spoke with Blue Cloud, one-on-one, it was as the result of a similar kind of spiritual ambush. David was reading the newspaper at the dining table, and I was pottering about the house when I noticed he looked unwell. He was resting his head in his hands and fidgeting in his chair. I put my hand on his shoulder.

"Are you okay?"

"I don't know what's wrong. I just don't feel right. It's like a pressure on my head and shoulders. I might sit in my office for a while. See if I can shift it."

David's office, or his mole-hole as I preferred to call it, was where he saw people for readings and spiritual healing. Unlike the average office, it had subdued lighting and a CD player to pipe meditation music, so it was a logical location to rest up and try to shift a headache.

He went in, and I continued with my jobs. I heard the music start, but a few minutes later as I passed the door, I noticed something else. Something strange; a deep, booming, slightly slurred voice. It was Blue Cloud.

I listened at the door, wondering who he was talking to and trying to make out what he was saying. Should I go in? I took the decision in haste, concluding he obviously wanted to say something to someone. I slowly opened the door. He was sitting up to the desk, cigarette in hand. The tape David used to record readings for people was running.

I slipped into the other chair, in awe but unafraid.

He was speaking into the microphone.

"We did not know, and yet we should, that you would come into our room this evening."
He had been recording a message for me; advice on how to help David in his quest to reach more people.
"Please remove the cigarette from the hand. He doesn't know we are here."

The cigarette that David had been smoking, had burned right down and was about to scorch his fingers. In those days, Blue Cloud's control of David's body was not so perfect, and he was unable to extinguish it. I took it from his fingers and stubbed it out, taking care not to touch him. I knew that to touch someone in trance without invitation could be dangerous for the medium, as well as disrespectful to the person in spirit. I don't pretend to understand the process of speaking through someone in this way, but I believe this could probably disrupt the flow of energy.

I am very fortunate that over the years I have spoken many times with my friend, as well as others from the high spirit realms. How many people have this opportunity?

Within the circle, the psychic energy we all have in our auras flows around the sitters and acts like a giant battery.

In this one-to-one scenario, the energy has to come from David and myself. Trance work always takes a physical toll on David, but especially so in these circumstances.

One evening, when the girls were small and before John was born, our close friend Maureen came to the house and we sat, in a group of three, speaking with those in spirit through David. About ten minutes in, we heard a terrible crash and a wail from upstairs. Our three-year-old daughter, Sian had fallen from the top bunk.

Mother's instinct kicked in and I rose and ran upstairs, without thinking. I picked her up and tried to console her, finally tucking her back into bed. When I arrived back downstairs I was horrified.

David was sprawled across the table making a terrible guttural sound. Poor Maureen was sitting opposite, looking helpless, and was obviously trying to direct some energy to him. I had broken the circle. I had not thought of it as a circle, because there were only three of us. It hadn't occurred to me that I couldn't leave.

I slipped back into my seat and desperately tried to restore the flow of energy which I had fractured. It took a while, and seeing him (I am still not sure who) struggle to regain some equilibrium was awful. It seemed that various personalities were stepping in and out to help him recover.

At last, David came around, disorientated and with an awful headache. It was such a relief to see him back. I tried to explain what I had done, but I don't think my words were registering. After a few minutes, he stood to go upstairs, but the problems didn't finish there. It was as though his spirit wasn't in sync with his body. Before our eyes, his feet began to miss the steps and he rolled over and over backwards, from the top of the stairs to the bottom. He could have broken his neck.

It was a stupid mistake, and one I never made again. Not everyone who spoke through in trance was from high spirit, but they always came for a reason. Usually, it was to teach something to the sitters, who were often too much in awe to ask questions. This may be why they sent Joey.

Before ever he spoke, David noticed Joey around the house. To start with, there was an odour. Often we find that spirit bring a smell for recognition. Usually, it will be their favourite flowers, perfume, or perhaps tobacco smoke. Joey's smell was not so pleasant – more like a recently used bathroom.

When he began to show himself, David wondered why he was hanging around. He was not from high spirit, nor did either of us know him. He looked around five-feet-five inches tall and had slicked back, thinning hair. His clothing was fairly smart but mismatched.

The next time I spoke to Blue Cloud, Joey took a trial

run at coming through. As I said, I don't understand the intricacies of the process, and obviously, at that time neither did he.

Blue Cloud spoke for around twenty minutes, then said goodnight, and quit David's body, but he didn't wake up. I could see someone else was trying to come through. I tried to direct more energy to him, but his whole body was vibrating. I had never seen that before. Suddenly, he fell forward, sprawling on the floor at my feet, only a couple of inches from the electric fire.

I knew I couldn't touch him without permission. I could only watch and wait as some controlling entity slowly reinstated David to his seat.

A few minutes later, I heard Joey's voice for the first time. A broad, black-country accent cursing and swearing; uncouth but not unfriendly.

"I thought I was on a bloody tractor, bouncing up an' down. What was all that about? I don't like this. They said, 'Get down there', and they shoved me down a bloody chimney or summat. They said it would help you and me. Now I don't know how to get out of here."

Although his maiden voyage was a disaster, Joey soon got the hang of it. When he spoke after that, it was to the circle. With practice, his coming and goings became smoother and his control improved.

People spoke to him more readily than to those from high spirit. He had only been over a few years and related more easily to the way people on earth think. We learned that he used to live between Dudley and Tipton, and had a wife, still living, called Linda.

Each circle we held was recorded on a Dictaphone, and later transcribed so that David could hear what had been said. In some instances, when Blue Cloud spoke, I acted as interpreter. Although he now has excellent control, his English, which he learned from a Frenchman, is not always clear. Being accustomed to the way he speaks, I stood a better chance of catching the harder words – although there were times when even I struggled to understand.

The strange thing is, when David listens to Blue Cloud's voice on tape, it does not sound the same as when he listens to him directly. Even BC has remarked that it doesn't sound like him. I can only presume there is some distortion when one uses vocal cords belonging to someone else.

Joey, despite the thick dialect, was more easily understood. He even learned to curb his colourful language when speaking to strangers. Questions were addressed to him without any hesitation, and conversation was usually relaxed, fruitful, and occasionally humorous.

I have chosen an excerpt from one of the transcribed

circles to give you some idea of his character. There are more transcripts in *'The Other Side; A Psychic's Story.'*

Joey;

Now I'm here. I'm not sure why. Perhaps it was just to catch him.
(David had started to fall forward after the previous person left his body abruptly.)
I've come through so you can bombard me with questions. You'll get sense out of me because I'm nearly as low as you lot. Ask me because I say it how it is. I call a spade a spade.

They're watching me. Every move I make. They're watching you too. It's like being on Big Brother, but it's not on channel 4. It's the Almighty Channel.
All these people watch and say, "What I would do now is…" But they aren't here. You are. You do it!

In the following section, Joey is referring to the seven levels of the spirit world, through which we hope to progress before reaching heaven.
Unless you are on 3 or 4, you are not very good. It doesn't look very good on 3 and 4 if you are on 7, but if you are low, it looks good. Fight for it and you will get it.

I'm going up. I'm learning a lot! Some of you are going down faster than I am going up.
(To a sitter) *I've seen your bedroom. Reminded me of when I was in Winson Green.*

(A prison in the West Midlands.)

When you die you have to account for yourself. I've accounted for myself and I went to 1, then 2, and now I've gone down to 1. (Reference to his progression in the levels of the spirit world.) *I'm climbing onto 2, I think.*

Sitter:
Now that you have passed over, has your spirit guide left you?

Joey:

He's still here. He talks to me now and again and teaches me now and again. He shows me things, but I've got to accept.
I could say, "I want you to go and live in Siberia," and you say, "I'm not doing that."
If your spirit guide tells you, and you think, "That is what I have to do. I don't want to do it, but I will." You are half-way there because you have done it but you didn't want to.

If, on the journey, you think, "I am doing some good here. I have done what high spirit want me to do and I am happy about it," you get some bonus points.

I am told things, and I think they must be right, but if I can't accept it I don't go higher. If it hasn't gone in, I'm not going to go up.
I'm questioning. It's not a bad thing to question, but right is right, and wrong is wrong.

I believe his purpose for visiting the circles was to help we sitters better understand, and to help himself progress at the same time.

Having passed over relatively recently, and being in the early stages of his progression, Joey's tone, as well as his degree of understanding, is noticeably different from when those from high-spirit speak. The following passage is taken from the transcript of a circle when Blue Cloud spoke. You might notice the difference, as he speaks with serenity and authority.

Blue Cloud:

Good evening my friends. (Evening and morning mean nothing to me, but I say 'good evening' because it is evening for you.) The moment you are born, you are on the road to die. Some people live a long, useless life.
Some people live a short, good life. You are here for a reason. When you finish your work, you go. Do what you can now. Always remember, there may not be a tomorrow.

A sitter asks about a dream where he seemed to visit the spirit world.

You astral project many times. We take you and show you many times, but where you visit may not be where you will go. We take you to see or to visit.
From time to time we will show you the way and we will show you where you go when you depart this world.

Sometimes you remember these times and sometimes you do not. When you depart from this world you will go towards the light. If, heaven forbid, you depart this world and find yourself in the dark, and you see a light, go toward the light and you will be helped over.

I must depart. The longer I stay, the weaker the body. Goodnight.
The blessings of The Almighty be with you.

Late one evening, I was talking to Blue Cloud in David's office. I suspect he tried to keep the noise down, but his voice is naturally resonant.

The following morning at breakfast, a gentleman who had travelled from Norway to receive spiritual healing and had stayed over at the hotel, told me that he had heard the big man talking in the night. As I brought him his toast, he told me he had come downstairs and listened at the door for a while.

I was mortified! How embarrassing! We had woken him up. I apologised unreservedly, offering compensation for his disturbed night.
"No, no, not at all!" he was very understanding. "It just reinforces the experience for me. It has shown me that all this is real. If this wasn't genuine, why would he go into trance when only his wife was there?"

That aspect hadn't occurred to me. I guess I have forgotten what it's like to think like a normal person.

Prophet of Doom?

Yes, I'm afraid he does tell people bad news. It may seem an obvious thing to say, but if you don't want to know – don't ask!

My apologies if you were hoping for a less brutal answer. In the early days, David hesitated before giving sensitive information, but he learned from experience, that if spirit were telling him to pass on a message, it was for good reason. You can be sure, he will tell you the truth, be it good or bad. He describes himself as a telephone between worlds. The phone conveys the message, without censoring the conversation. He has complete trust in Blue Cloud, whose job is to facilitate people in spirit coming through, and he has faith that everything conveyed is done so for a reason - even if he cannot for the life of him, see what that reason might be.

When David was in good health, he travelled extensively, both in the UK and overseas. He worked on stage, TV, and radio. While he appreciated that this was an effective way to get the message across to large groups of people, he suffered greatly with his nerves, and although he disguised it well, always hated walking out in front of an audience. I travelled with him when possible, taking care of the trivial stuff, like ensuring the sound system was working or handling his diary.

At one such event, I remember a group of girls were sitting at the front of the auditorium. Many people come to see David for help and advice or to seek comfort after a bereavement. Others buy a ticket, simply out of curiosity or for a bit of fun. I judged these young ladies to be in the latter category. They looked to be in their twenties and were giggling behind their drinks. Nice girls, but obviously there purely for entertainment purposes. I have no objection to this. It can be satisfying to see people walk away, amazed and surprisingly receptive to ideas they would not have previously entertained; newly aware that their actions will determine their fate in another world.

David pointed to one of their number, a pretty blonde girl with a nice smile.
"The young lady in the pink top."
She raised her glass, blonde hair falling from its clip as she nodded her head to acknowledge him.
"Yes, you," he continued, but then he fell silent. I saw him tilt his head, listening to the silent voice at his shoulder, then he met her gaze, took a breath, and continued. "I'm sorry. I have to say this. You look very well and happy, but I am being told that you only have a matter of weeks or months to live."

There was an audible gasp in the room. It was a shocking thing to hear. All eyes were on the young lady. Her friends stared at her, open-mouthed, as she self-consciously wiped away the tear that was forming, although her smile remained.
"Do you understand what I am saying?"

The girl nodded, then answered quietly. "Thank you."
"Don't thank me!" David was emotional now, "I have just told you that you are going to die – and I'm afraid it will be soon!"

The friend to her right was openly sobbing. The one on her left took her hand, and they exchanged a knowing glance.
"I know that I don't have long." The girl spoke again, "I came here tonight, not knowing what to believe. If you had told me anything else, I wouldn't have believed in you, or in a life after this one. Now I know you are genuine, and I know I don't have to be afraid. Thank you so much."

It took a moment or two for David to compose himself. The audience was emotional, but all eyes were on him. I could see he was struggling, but he managed to carry on, giving the girl a comforting message from her grandmother to affirm the truth of an afterlife.

These gifts can be a curse for a sensitive man. David feels for people, very deeply. Perhaps this is why they used to call mediums 'sensitives'. I expect it is a pre-requisite of the job. He could easily have swerved this difficult message; moved on to the next person for fear of upsetting the girl. If he had, she would have left without the knowledge she so desperately needed at that time. I can't count the times I have witnessed David cheerfully wave a client off, then burst into tears when the door closes. He has shown them their loved one lives on, but he can't bring them back.

No-one's life can be sunshine all the time, but after a rainstorm comes the petrichor, that fresh, musky smell of renewal. Then comes the realization that it is the way of all things, and must ever be so. Birth, love, death, loss, rebirth; life rumbles on as God intended.

One cannot always distinguish good news from bad. If a girl is pregnant, is that good or bad? If you are getting divorced, is that good or bad? David just tells people what he is shown, confident in the knowledge that everything is for a reason.

When it comes to more general advice about the future, spirit can see the path that we are on, and may be able to warn us of impending disaster, but we have our free will and we choose our own direction. Our lives are not pre-determined. We can veer off course and make disastrous decisions. Spirit would not predict bad news without also giving the advice needed to either deal with the situation or change it.

Admittedly, on occasion, David does try to wrap the truth up. Sometimes a message requires a well-thought-out, more tactful presentation.

For example, an elderly lady came to see him privately for spiritual healing. She was living in a care home, and suffered from chronic pain from crippling arthritis, to the extent that her daughter, suspecting she was giving up, brought her to David after hearing him speak on a radio show.

The old lady sat in David's healing room, and he

stood before her, placing his hands on hers. The warmth and vibration generated by the healing, flowed into her gnarled fingers, and she began to smile gently.

When the session finished, she was peaceful and in better spirits. She sat in silence for a few minutes before she spoke.
"Please tell me, Mr. Drew, after seeing you today will I be pain-free."

David raised his eyes and, behind her head, saw curtains closing, the symbol of an imminent passing. He took her hand, looked into her eyes, and said, "Believe me, before long you will be free of any pain."

She squeezed his hand and thanked him. He likes to think that she knew what he was saying.

Spiritual healing is not the same as faith healing, because no faith is required. The healing energy comes from God and is transmitted via His ministering angels, to doctors and helpers in the spirit world, who in turn, pass it on to the healer, who administers it to the person in need.

When people receive healing from David, who is simply a link in this chain, they often remark on feeling a soothing heat and vibration from his hands. Sometimes they see colours, especially shades of green.

Some people also feel a second pair of invisible hands on their body, perhaps their head or ankles as spirit doctors work on them.

Everyone receives some benefit from the healing, and many receive a long-lasting cure, even small babies and animals, who have no faith.

There are times when people can't travel to see David. Then absent-healing can be administered. In this way, even those who are unaware, may receive healing at the request of another. The healing energy is then conveyed, by the doctor in spirit, directly to the recipient, at the direction of the healer who received the request.

Sometimes the patient is completely unaware, but often they have strange sensations or experiences while the healing is taking place. Some close their eyes and see a face, or feel heat or the touch of hands.

When Tim was a teenager, he tore a cartilage in his knee while playing football. There was a long wait for the operation, and it was very painful, so David decided to help. Knowing that Tim, though fascinated, was nervous of the spirit world, he decided to arrange for him to receive absent-healing without knowing it was taking place. It didn't quite work out that way.

The following morning David was forced to confess what he had done. During the night, Tim had felt himself being lifted out of his body, suspended over the bed, while invisible hands manipulated his knee. Such a drastic experience is quite unusual, and he was absolutely terrified, but the good news was, he no longer needed the operation.

If someone has a health problem, David is often shown this as a dark patch in the aura around the affected area. Sometimes he simultaneously feels pain. He will advise that the person visit a doctor to address the problem, and offer healing in addition, especially when earthly doctors can no longer help.

Many medics who have passed on, choose to continue their work by administering spiritual healing. Since I have been with David, several spirit doctors have worked with him, each one specialising in a specific area.

When he was running the Psychic Club in Lytham-St-Annes, guest mediums would visit, either to demonstrate or simply observe. One evening, after David had been working on stage, a lady pulled him to one side and explained she had seen Albert Schweitzer standing at his side.

This was an interesting development. He had indeed been joined by a new doctor, who had introduced himself as Dr. Albert but said little else. Her description matched him perfectly, but although David had heard the name, neither of us knew who Albert Schweitzer was, or what he looked like.

The next time David saw the good doctor, he asked

him why he had not mentioned who he was. His reply epitomized his character.

"It is not the worker who is important, but the work that must be done."

He was reluctant to talk about himself, so we made some enquiries, (remember, these were the days before Google), and discovered that he had been a missionary, a doctor, musician, and Nobel Peace Prize winner, who worked in Africa, building hospitals to help the lepers.

We were told he was represented in Blackpool's waxworks museum, so one afternoon we made our way to the promenade and took the family there for an outing.

The exhibit was quite easily located. As we peered at his likeness, he leaned over David's shoulder.

"It was 1965."

The plaque said he died in 1969.

Dr. Albert is always keen to work, to the extent, he would have driven David day and night if he could.

Their working relationship flourished, and each became accustomed to the other's ways, perfectly in step like some synchronized spiritual foxtrot.

As quiet meditation music played, David would place his hands over the patient, as Albert, sharing his space, placed ghostly hands over his.

Before long, the spirit doctor decided he preferred to take, quite literally, a more hands-on approach. David would begin the healing process, standing by the patient, and wake up some time later, sitting at his desk. At first, he was confused and disorientated, then he realised that he had been taken into trance.

He accepted that Dr. Albert preferred to work this way, but it was sometimes awkward when the patient asked questions afterwards about something he had said.

When Dr. Albert had been with him for a few years, David was approached by the widow of a healer whom Albert previously worked with.

Joyce Leslie, a lovely lady from Brighton on the south coast, saw a magazine article about David's healing work and asked if he would meet with her. It seems, after her husband John died, the good doctor needed to find a new channel so he could continue his spiritual healing work. The dates matched up perfectly to when he joined David's team.

She invited David to her home, some forty-seven miles from London, where her late husband had worked from his healing room. When they entered his office, she reached up to a high shelf and took down a miniature bust of Dr. Albert, passing it to David. It had been presented to John by the Albert Schweitzer Trust when he visited Alsace.

She said she missed Dr. Albert's company very much,

and it was only right that the statue be passed on to his new place of work.

Everyone dies eventually. It stands to reason that some people who come for healing will not receive a complete and lasting cure, although all do experience some benefit, perhaps pain relief or improvement of symptoms.

All things for a reason, but despite all his wisdom, it takes an immense emotional toll on David on the rare occasion that someone he has been desperate to help, passes away.

When a person dies, their spirit leaves the body behind, and they may be greeted by relatives and friends who passed on before them, but the experience is not the same for everyone. The way we die, and the condition of our body, can affect our mental attitude to our passing.

An elderly person may slip in and out of their body as they prepare to leave it for good. Each time they do so, the silver cord erodes a little. They may see loved ones in the spirit world, who have come to help them with their transition. This will be a very different experience from the person who dies suddenly in an accident. The silver cord breaks and the spirit is suddenly released from their body without warning, which can be very confusing for them. Often they don't initially realise they have died.

In every case, adjusting to your new surroundings is a slow process. At some point, your life will be studied, usually with the help of your spirit guide, and your mistakes will be pointed out. In due course, your level of spirituality will determine your place in the spirit world, and you will find yourself in your new home. From here you will rise or fall, depending on your character.

Once we have vacated our body, its constraints are forgotten as we start our exciting journey. It is no longer of use to us, and we cast it aside like an old coat. It may, however, be useful in helping someone else to live and learn on the earth. David and I have both registered for our organs to be donated for transplant upon our death.

On Tour

Haunted Chester

Healing

With Dr. Albert

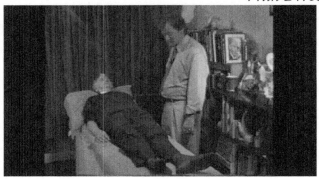

Home Life

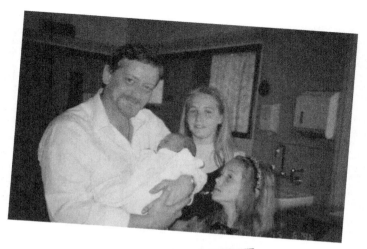

Igor in his prime

David relaxes with Mark and John

With Maureen and Ricky

Father of the Bride

The Drew Clan Today

Last Night I Had a Vivid Dream;
Could it have been real?

Perchance to Dream.

My maternal grandmother understood the value of dreams. She would have learned this from her mother, who, lying in bed one night, heard her son, Bill, (away fighting in WWI) shout up to the bedroom window.

Thinking he had unexpectedly come home on leave, she ran downstairs, and out into the garden, but there was no-one there. It seemed so real that she couldn't accept it had just been a dream.

She later learned that Bill, (my grandma's eldest brother), still overseas, was shot at the same time she heard the shout.

My grandma was born in 1896 and she grew up in Lound, North Nottinghamshire. In this small village, a trip to buy provisions required a five-mile walk to the nearest town. She was making this journey one summer afternoon when the birdsong was disturbed by the rumble of a horse and trap thundering behind her. The lane being narrow, she stepped sideways into a gap in the tall hedge, to allow it to pass. The ground trembled and the wind tousled her hair as the carriage rushed by.

When she stepped back into the lane, which stretched straight ahead for miles, it was silent and completely deserted.

Back home that night, she told her family what had happened. To her parents, the story was familiar. It seems she had encountered the famous Mab Lane Ghost. The phantom carriage was periodically sighted by locals as it careered down the well-travelled dirt road.

I am sure most families have inherited a ghost story or two. These visions and experiences are more common than you may think, largely because, for fear of ridicule, people are selective regarding who they share their stories with. I have heard many haunting tales in David's waiting room, each whispered like an embarrassing secret. When faced with someone who is likely to believe them, even the most grounded person is eager to offload.

My grandma was no stranger to premonitions and was known to hear two phantom knocks to indicate an imminent passing. It was often followed by the same ominous nightmare. There would be a social gathering, where one family member or friend was missing. No-one knew where the person was, and she was never able to find them. Within a matter of weeks, this person would inevitably take ill and die.

Incidentally, the tradition appears to carry on through the generations.

Ayesha heard the famous knocks, which herald a passing in our family, on the evening *after* her father-in-law died.

"You're late!" She said - and heard a phantom chuckle.

Of course, not all dreams are meaningful. Some are simply the waste product of a sleeping brain, but the others, the special ones, can be quite extraordinary.

When my mother was pregnant with my eldest brother, she had a vivid and disturbing dream in which she was wandering the halls of a tall, vaulted building with stone pillars and high, arched windows. As she strolled around, she became aware of her hand brushing against something icy-cold. She turned to see what it was, and saw her father, dead and laid out on a stone slab. My father woke to find her crying hysterically beside him. It took him some time to convince her that her dad was safe, well, and asleep in the next room.

Three weeks later, he was taken ill and died unexpectedly; destined never to meet his first grandchild.

You can usually tell when a dream is meaningful. There is something poignant about the significant ones, although not all are so easily deciphered. Sometimes, dreams which seem to carry a dire portent, are misinterpreted. Mum's dream was quite literal, but often there is a less obvious, symbolic meaning.

For example, a death can signify casting off your old way of life in favour of a new beginning, or even news of a birth.

Often, when those in the spirit world try to give us a more intricate message, it can be better conveyed as a story; a parable style omen for us to evaluate and translate for ourselves.

When I was seventeen, in those simple times before the advent of mobile phones, I lived alone in my pokey, Blackpool apartment. Around this time, I had an unusually vivid dream. I was trapped inside a huge, glass dome. In there with me was a lion. On the outside of the dome, I could see my dad. He was present, but couldn't reach me. It was a vivid and terrifying dream which stayed with me for a few days, until its meaning was revealed.

My father lived in our home-town of Retford, which was almost three-hundred miles away. I would trek to the telephone box two or three times a week, to call him.

One cold afternoon I was chatting to him from the kiosk at the end of my street. In those days it was not unusual for a queue to form at these boxes, so when I noticed a man in a duffle coat, standing close up against the glass, I paid little attention.

I turned with my back to him, determined not to be rushed. As I did so, he moved to the other side of the cubicle, so that he remained in my peripheral vision. I turned again, and he repeated the maneuver. That was when I realised he was exposing himself. My mind raced as I tried to keep my voice calm. I hoped that he would move on, but as time passed it became clear he had no intention of going anywhere.

Continuing my conversation as if nothing was wrong, I mentally planned the safest method of exiting the box. There was no point in alarming my dad. There was nothing he could do and he had a bad heart. I decided to wind-up the conversation and leave swiftly, hoping the man would allow me to pass. I hung-up and pushed against the heavy door to make my escape, but he was ready and forced me back inside.

Now I was face to face with my captor. He was much taller than I, unshaven and around thirty. I could smell alcohol and the damp of his woolen overcoat. In a pathetic attempt to defend myself, I reached up and sank my fingernails into his cheek. He looked startled but determined as he spoke.
"I'm not going to hurt you."
I replied with faux confidence, roaring like a new-born tiger-cub facing a hunter. "I know you're not!"

I thank God for what happened next.

As he pushed me back inside, I managed to keep one foot jammed in the heavy door, close to the strong spring of the hinge.

This meant that the door remained slightly open behind him, but from my position near the fulcrum, I couldn't open it further. Then, from the street, I heard a shout.

"Excuse me mate. Do you know how I get to Church Street?"

A lorry-driver, presuming we were a couple, had pulled over to ask directions. Flustered, the man left me, and went over to talk to him as though nothing was wrong.

Adrenaline pumping, I took my chance and flew up the hill like an Olympic sprinter. In around three minutes I was at my front door, looking over my shoulder, the key rattling in the lock. My dream came flooding back. The lion was the embodiment of danger. The glass dome equated to the glass phone booth, and my dad being there but not able to help, was self-evident.

I am sure the lorry-driver was influenced to call out at that moment. How likely is it for someone in a vehicle to ask directions from two people inside a phone booth, even if the door isn't quite shut? I felt blessed that day to have received, not just a warning, but also a rescue.

The lion has since featured many times in my dreams, each time as a representation of danger. This kind of reverie is a nod to the future; a warning to prepare us; a tip-off from above.

Not all significant dreams take the form of a warning. My favourites are the ones where we meet with our loved ones or travel in this world and even in the next.

Your loved ones can come to you in your sleep. Although not every dream you have of them will be real, you will probably sense when there is more substance to it.

It is possible to have conversations you thought you would never again be able to share. Alas, you may not remember all of these meetings, and some aspects may become confused, but something usually remains on a subconscious level. Blue Cloud once told me that when we dream it is as though information is poured into the sponge of our minds. Upon waking, the sponge is squeezed and we forget some of the experience; lose some of the knowledge we absorbed. It is a good idea to keep a notebook by your bed to make a record of anything you can recall before it is lost forever.

Once I had a vivid dream in which I was playing a beautiful, Native American drum. It was exquisitely painted and had such a sweet, mellow tone. A few days afterwards, we sat in circle and Blue Cloud asked me if I liked my present. I was able to thank him in person. This was confirmation to me that it had been more than just a dream.

This was not the only gift he gave me. In a similar way, he presented me with a blanket he made especially for me. It is protective, radiant, and comforting, and when I need it, I feel it around my shoulders.

The process of writing this book has inspired me to sort through old papers, videos, and audio recordings of circles. In doing so I found a tape whose transcript I have decided, after some deliberation, to include. Its content is quite personal to me, but it perhaps gives a window into my world; a taste of the weird and wonderful life of the psychic's wife.
Blue Cloud Begins.

"My Jane, I have a little present for you. Bear with me, please. This is very difficult. Two peoples will very quickly say hello to you. Two peoples very close to you. This is very difficult and.. this will not be easy. We try for you."

Next on the tape, after a minute or two, my grandma's voice.

"Janey! It's me! Jane! It's Grandma. Sending love to you. Love to your mum. She's a fool sometimes, but I love her. I love you."

"Are you happy?" I ask

"Very. Very happy. Very happy."

"I'm sorry we never got to say goodbye."
"Easier for me." She pauses, her voice getting weaker. *"Until we meet again."*

Three or four minutes pass before the next voice, which I don't recognise.

"God in the highest glory....be with you."

"Who is it?" I ask

"Maria."

Sister Maria is my spirit guide, whose voice I had never heard.
"Thank you for speaking to me."

"I thank the Lord that He has allowed me to guide you through.
You were a sister before. You did not know, but there is no reason why you should not know. You are more at home in the Cathedral. On the Earth plane, I married Christ our Lord. Do you understand? So did you, on the Earth plane before."

"Did we know each other then?"

"Yes, we were good chums, but that was to be my last time." Another pause.
"I am always with you. I give you what help I can so that in return, you can help.
Never say, 'This is what I want.' Always say, 'What may I do.
May God be with you."

I was grateful for this wonderful gift and so very aware of my privilege. Few people find themselves in a position to receive such an opportunity.

When my grandmother died, my mother could never forgive herself that she wasn't with her at the end. She lived close by, on the corner of our street, and my mum saw her almost every day of her life, but on the weekend when she was unexpectedly taken ill and died, we were away on a mini-break. Before we left, Mum called in to say goodbye, while we waited in the car. I didn't even go inside. Other than commenting that she had a tummy ache, Grandma was fine. We set off for two days in Blackpool.

There was no way to reach us when she took ill that evening. We came home, as planned, the day after, and Mum went straight to her house, bearing gifts. Her brother was waiting to tell her their mum had passed away in the night. It was a terrible shock and she bore this guilt for years, until my grandma came to her in a dream one night and told her simply, 'Let it be'.

To hear my grandmother say it was easier for her, made me think. Those left behind tend to dwell on the last time they saw their loved one; the last thing they said, but for those in spirit, it is not the last time they will see you. It is as though the plug is pulled in the middle of a really bad day.

On any other day, all negative situations would be forgotten and everyone would go back to normal soon after, but when someone has died, that doesn't happen.

Our perception is that the relationship was frozen on that day, and regrets hang heavy. From the spirit world, however, they have a greater understanding. From their perspective, the plug wasn't pulled at all.

Some years after her passing, I had a strangely clear dream about my grandma.

I was approaching the gate to her house. When I looked up I saw her walking along the garden path, holding my little dog, who she had always been very fond of.

In the dream, I was aware that she was dead, and we had a lovely chat, catching up on things and eventually parting with a hug. I awoke, exhilarated by the feeling that I had actually been with her.

I mentioned the dream to my dad. He surmised that she had probably been on my mind because it was her birthday. The problem with this explanation is, I had no idea that it *was* her birthday.

At the time of writing it is less than a year since I lost my mum. In our relationship, as is often the way, I went from child to friend to parent. Strange how everything in life turns full circle. I hope I was as caring to her at the end of her life as she was to me at the beginning of mine. She lived for her children, grandchildren, and great-grandchildren, and was intrinsically maternal.

I did my best to be what she needed, but, just like

parenthood, there isn't a manual. We just have to try our best and hope we get some of it right. It was sad to see her spark fade, but we always managed to have a laugh, even in difficult circumstances.

I arrived home after visiting her one day and realised I had forgotten my mobile phone. When I went back to collect it, she was waiting, "You left your phone. I tried to call you to tell you, but you didn't answer. It keeps making a noise and flashing."

When I picked it up there were six missed calls and a text – all from her.

At her annual Parkinson's appointments, they would always give her a memory test. We would be escorted to a room where a specialist nurse would talk her through the standard form.

"I am going to tell you five words that I want you to remember. Then I will ask you some questions, and at the end I want you to tell me what those five words were. Ready? Banana; Church; Red; Goat; Dress." The lady was very kind. "Now, repeat them back to me twice, and try to remember them."

Mum complied with good grace.

So far so good. She then asked her to count backwards from one hundred in increments of nine. She did this faster than I could do it in my head.

Draw a clock and a cube. What is the day and the date? Who is the prime minister? She aced the test.

"That was wonderful Mrs. Littlewood. Now, can you tell me those five words I asked you to remember at the beginning?"

"What five words?"

"The five words I asked you to remember at the beginning."

Mum looked to me for help.

"Okay, I will give you a clue. There was a colour."

"Yellow." Mum guessed.

"A fruit then?"

"Strawberry."

I tried to make a joke of things because it was the best way for us both to cope.

"Will you be kind to me if I go bonkers?" she sometimes asked. I would reply, "I am, aren't I?" and we would both laugh.

I don't want to give the impression that my mum wasn't intelligent. She was perhaps not as erudite as my dad, but she was razor-sharp and witty. She was eloquent and even had poems published. Age and illness took their toll, but the important stuff never left her. In latter days, she might have referred to her glaucoma drops as 'eye tablets' and the fan as the 'air lamp', but she always knew who we all were, and loved us fiercely.

She could see the humour in her mistakes, in fact, she was quite the giggler. I remember her hilarity when she called someone in to replace her smoke alarm because it was beeping, only to find it had been a fault with her hearing aid.

More poignantly, she took my hand one day and looked at me with worried eyes. "What if I forget you?" She implored.
"Don't worry." I said, "*I* won't forget *you*!"

Most of us encounter death before it comes to take us. Like a storm, we see it coming and nothing can stop it. I was there for my mum at the end and held her hand as she passed.
I tried to comfort her, telling her she needn't be afraid - that she would go to sleep and wake up feeling better. The student nurse shot me a look, but it wasn't a lie.

I waited until I was sure she had passed before allowing myself to fall apart.

Grief is a difficult burden to bear, but it doesn't weigh us down forever. If you imagine we enter this world through one gate, and leave through another, our life is the journey between the two. When we lose someone, grief is padlocked around us like a bolder on a great chain.

Each morning we take a step. At first, it is hard to move forward and we may feel like giving up, but as we drag the rock, little pieces chip away and it begins to slowly erode.

With every step, it gets smaller until, despite pulling this weight, we are able to complete our daily tasks. The burden is always there, but it gets smaller and smaller as we walk. When at last we reach our destination, we find a key hanging on the gate. Only then we can open the padlock and release the weight, and we pass through the gate where our loved ones wait. If we give up and sit down, instead of moving forward, the rock does not wear away and we never reach that key. We have to keep moving. One step at a time.

Since she passed, David has seen my mum two or three times, and I met up with her once in a dream.

It can take a little while after someone passes for them to learn how to communicate, so I am very lucky to have seen her so soon. The dream was incredibly vivid, and I have not the slightest doubt she was really there.

In my dream, the day was bright and pleasant. I was walking along a grassy river-bank when from behind I heard Mum's voice calling my name. I turned, but couldn't see her. I continued to walk, wondering if it had been my imagination. It had been so long since I heard her voice. Then I heard it again. The familiar sound I thought I had forgotten.

This time I saw her, quite a distance away down the path. She was stepping backwards, hastening away from a woman in a long robe, who appeared to be talking to her.

At last, she broke away, turned, and ran toward me. Although she passed at age eighty-nine, she now looked around fifty as she skipped effortlessly toward me. Her mobility and hearing were completely restored. If we die when we are elderly, in the spirit world we gradually begin to look younger, until we appear to be around thirty-three. (It may be significant that Jesus was thirty-three when he died.) It was a long time since I had seen her so animated. She was her old self.

We hugged and she beamed happily, telling me she missed me and apologising for making me wait.
"I had to wait for her to step back." She added, motioning to where the woman had been standing.
I got the impression that this was someone from high spirit - perhaps her guide, who was helping her with the logistics of the visit.

We chatted excitedly and I asked if she had been to see my brother, Al. She said she had, and remarked that he had been having his dinner outside. Then I asked if she had visited my other brother, Paul. She told me to tell him she was going to see him next. She mentioned seeing David sitting up to a table in front of some dark curtains, with a carrier bag at his feet. We had moved house since she passed, and this sounded exactly like his new favourite spot.

Next, she spoke about her time in hospital, how awful she had felt, how she could never get comfortable.

She was pleased that terrible time was behind her. Having been immobile for so long, things were much better for her now. As we talked, I noticed her hearing had been restored.

All too soon, it was time for her to go, and we parted on the promise that she would be back as soon as she could. I awoke, remembering every detail of our meeting, as elated as if I had seen her in the flesh.

When I told Al, it made perfect sense to him. A few weeks earlier, when on holiday in Rome, he had a strong feeling that Mum was with him. He was sitting at a pavement café at the time, or as she would have more simply put it, 'having his dinner outside.'

I know that both of my parents come to see their brood from time to time.

A few months after Dad died, I had a strange and vivid dream that I was walking around Blue Cloud Lodge. As I tried to turn the lights on, my hand glided through the switches as if I was a ghost. Passing the doorway to the bar, I caught sight of a figure sitting up to the round table by the window. It was my dad.

This was not the kind of dream where you are unaware your loved one is dead. We both knew that he had passed, and greeted each other with joy to be reunited. He was relaxed and spoke calmly about events that took over him before he died, and I told him what had been happening in my life.

I don't remember the detail of the conversation, but he was, as always, philosophical and warm.

As we were saying our goodbyes, a strange thing happened. Sian, who was about eight at the time, appeared on the stairs in her pyjamas. She was rubbing her eyes and crying. It was as if she was confused and astral travelling. Her granddad took hold of her hand and addressed her in the teasing way I had forgotten he had with children.
"Hey, hey! What are you laughing at? I heard you both in your bedroom before. You were grunting like a pig."

The dream faded and I woke. Could Sian have been astral travelling? It was so real, and yet the part about the pig didn't fit. It made me doubt its veracity.

At breakfast, I spoke to Ayesha, who shared a room with Sian but was three years older.

"I hope you girls went straight to sleep and didn't stay up playing last night."
"Not for long Mum. We were just joking around for a bit. We were pretending to be Andy's mum."
Andy was a school friend.
"Why on earth would you do that?"
"When she laughs she makes a snorting noise. It sounds really funny. Like a pig."

I scolded them for being rude, secretly pleased at hearing the evidence for my dream being real.

Some dreams are destined to remain a mystery. I must quickly mention one strange dream that I don't completely understand. David was in the pub at the time, and I had gone to bed early.

In my nightmare, the house was in darkness and I could hear there was an intruder. I was frozen with fear, knowing the children were asleep in the next room.

These were the days before everyone on the planet had a mobile phone. I crept to the house phone, desperate not to be discovered, and dialed the number of our local pub. I knew it by heart, but every time I tried to call, it either didn't ring at all or it rang and no-one answered. I concentrated hard and dialed each number carefully and deliberately, time and time again. I was frantic but no-one answered. I woke in a cold sweat. It was eleven pm.

At ten-to-eleven they rang the bell for last orders in the pub. The bar was crowded as people rushed to buy their last drinks.

David was seated at the bar when the phone began to ring. For some reason, he became concerned and thought it might be me. It was a strange thing to surmise, but he couldn't get it out of his head.
It rang and rang, but no one picked up. David was unsettled, but at last, the ringing stopped.

Then it started again. He called out to the barman. "Can you get that phone?"

"We're a bit busy Dave," the man shouted back, as he totted up a large round.

The phone rang three or four times. It finally stopped as they called time at eleven pm. - exactly the time I woke up

Coincidence? Maybe, but life with David has taught me to keep an open mind. There are very few coincidences.

When we are relaxed in our beds, just waking up or about to go to sleep, this is the time we are most receptive to spiritual influence. We peep through that gap between dream and reality, to glimpse a brief snapshot of another world. You may see a figure by your bed, or feel someone hold your hand. I remember one night as I was falling asleep, I saw a line of nuns by the side of my bed. I closed my eyes, presuming it was my imagination, then opened them with a start when I felt one of them touch my cheek.

Recurring dreams plague us because we are not grasping something that spirit are trying to say. The message is repeated, either until we understand or it is no longer relevant. I had one such nightmare throughout my childhood. It played out like this.

My mother would be washing-up at the kitchen sink, as the clock on the mantle chimed. I knew this sound was a signal that something was coming to get me, and I would quickly conceal myself in the nearest available hiding place.

Once out of sight, holding my breath, I would hear the door open, and sometimes catch a glimpse of the legs of a giant as he stomped around the house, trying to find me. After a while, the clock would chime again, indicating it was time for him to leave. I would wake-up, heart banging but relieved to be safe.

The very last time I had this dream I would have been about fifteen, and it was different. I was hiding behind the armchair as the giant searched the house, but this time, when the clock struck the hour and it was time for him to leave, he became angry, throwing things in his frustration. I could hear furniture crashing around, then to my horror, he picked up the armchair, revealing my hiding place.

I closed my eyes and held still, afraid of what was to come, but the giant immediately calmed himself, pleased perhaps, that I was found at last.
Lifting me, high above his head, he carried me out of my home, across brilliant green fields and shimmering blue rivers. It was exciting and even pleasant. I wondered, at that moment, why, for all those years, I had lived in fear of him.

I now see this as the overture to meeting David, and the giant as a representation of Blue Cloud, waiting to bring us together when the time was right.

His size, appearance and the idea of change were frightening, but in reality, there was nothing to fear.

Although people often ask David to interpret their dreams, usually the best person to do this is the dreamer. The message is meant for you, geared around your experience and your understanding of the situation. If you apply some thought, you can usually crack the code yourself.

Does He Know What You Are Thinking?

Look Into My Eyes.

Having psychic ability is not the same as being a mind reader. David can't tell what you are thinking. It could appear this way at times, as he may well know your state of mind or your current situation. He is able to see if you are troubled or worried; happy or ill; angry or head-over-heels in love. Everything is there in your aura if he is interested enough to take a look. I'm afraid there are few secrets, but he is not tuning-in to your thoughts.

The aura is a glow of energy, the life force that surrounds all living things, including us. David calls it the clothing of the spirit. He sees it as layered clouds of coloured light. There are two ways in which this force betrays our condition. The first is by hue. The shades of colour all have a meaning. For more detail on this, David's first book, *'Stairway to Heaven'* goes into depth regarding the language of the aura. For example, a bright-red tinge tells of energy and determination, and a rosy-red shows love. Pale yellow is a spiritual colour, while a mustard-yellow indicates someone untrustworthy. Leaf-green is a healing colour, indicative of a considerate nature, but a dark, dull green reveals a jealous heart. A grey patch within the aura is a negative sign. It shows illness in that area, or confusion and depression if it sits around the head.

The second way your aura speaks to David is via the signs and symbols that it contains. Spirit use it like a chalk-board, to communicate with you, through him. For example, a tree branching in two directions depicts a parting of the ways – a breakup or bereavement perhaps, and a triangle is a warning of danger. A simple, yet effective system which enables him to evidence his authenticity to the sitter and advise them on the future.

In addition to seeing your emotions and personality within the aura, people in spirit also tell him things. This is useful if you are having a psychic reading. Not so much when you are married to him and just had a covert spending spree in River Island, or indeed are trying in vain to conceal his birthday present.

He hears the voice either objectively, that is to say as a tangible voice in the room, or sometimes subjectively, as a voice in his head. It is often faint and crackly, like an old radio. The person wishing to communicate may choose to use the psychic energy available to show themselves, rather than speak. In this case, they will portray themselves in such a way so that when he describes the person, you will recognize them - perhaps with a walking-stick or a pipe. In some cases, they are able to both speak and show themselves. The confusion comes when the voice he hears does not belong to the person he is seeing. This is something he needs to watch out for.

When David is asked if he sees spirit '*all the time*', he explains by likening it to being in a room where the

TV is constantly on in the corner. Although the program is on, you can be having a conversation or reading the newspaper without paying any attention. If someone asks, "What is this show?" you focus on the television and tell them.

The word 'psychic' is little understood and can cover a multitude of misconceptions. Some presume David to be a magician or a hypnotist. We had one relative who used to turn his photo to the wall before she got undressed, just in case he could see her. The truth is that he is merely extra sensitive to spiritual influences.

Despite all this intuitive knowledge, the one thing David is apt to be strangely blind to is when someone is attracted to him. I am not sure if this has anything to do with the 'not seeing things for himself' scenario, but I think it more likely that, like many other men, he is simply obtuse when it comes to understanding the fairer sex.

I had to accustom myself quite early on, to the amount of female attention being an attractive and caring psychic medium attracts. Over the years, David has had his fair share of stalkers; women crouching behind our car on the driveway; accidentally bumping into him in his local pub (which is a good hour's drive from where they live); that kind of thing.

The writing on the wall came one evening when we were newly married. In those days, David would conduct 'party bookings'. This is the name we used when a group of people met at a house, having booked him to give individual psychic readings to their guests. They were often women, and wine and snacks were usually abundant in the anteroom, where they nervously waited to go through for their private reading. Think of a more exciting version of a Tupperware Party – or a less exciting Ann Summers.

This particular evening, the booking had been in Lostock Hall, Greater Manchester. We were living in Blackpool at that time, and an exhausted David arrived home at midnight, having driven for an hour in the pouring rain. Each time he gives a reading, it saps his strength, like draining a battery. (We eventually realised that to do one reading after another in this way was detrimental to his health, and changed the way he worked, limiting the number of people he saw per day and spacing them more efficiently.)

As he put the key in the door that night, the phone was ringing. The lateness of the call should have been a clue. It was one of the women who had attended the party booking, wanting to book an event at her own house in the same neighborhood. A date was agreed for around a month later.

That date quickly came around, but the naïve David was puzzled by what he found when he arrived at the address.

The young woman showed him into a dimly lit room,

where he was the only guest. Presuming the others were yet to arrive, he asked where she wanted him to sit. She indicated the vacant seat next to her on the sofa. As they chatted, he noticed the romantic music playing and began to suspect an ulterior motive. "When will the others be arriving?"

"You don't have to worry," she slid closer, "my husband works nights."

That was it! Like a frightened rabbit, he was up and out the door like the true Don Juan he has always been.

As soon as he got home he told me what had happened, unsure if he had misread the signs, asking for reassurance and relieved to be safely back at home. I thought it was funny. Until five am.

We were both sound asleep when the telephone rang. At that time of day, you always think the worst, so, in a daze, I jumped out of bed and took the call. A female voice asked to speak to David. I explained he was asleep, but she pleaded, saying she just needed to hear the sound of his voice. I rolled my eyes, but obliged and woke him up. He was kind to her but afterwards asked me not to do that again.

The phone rang every half-hour throughout the night.

People get crushes on their doctors and psychiatrists all the time. For similar reasons, some people become attached after David has helped them, perhaps through a difficult period in their lives, but it is not healthy for them to rely on him too heavily.

He always says he is here to be used as a signpost, not a crutch.

He is here to help people, and I am here to support him. I do understand how people can become confused, and I can see why anyone would love him, but I have never felt threatened by his admirers. Neither of us are perfect, but I always knew we were perfect for each other.

Strange or Wonderful?

At theatres and conference halls when David was on stage, it would always provoke a giggle when he announced to the audience, "When I was young, people thought I was crazy. As I grew older, I wondered if they might be right. Now I *know* that I'm crazy, it's no problem."

Our friends tend to fall into two categories. Of course, they all know about David's gifts, but there are those who never mention it, apart from the occasional, 'You should have seen that coming' joke. (Surprisingly though, many of these secretly have faith in his abilities, and unexpectedly turn up on the doorstep to see David when they need help.) Such friends often have lighthearted nicknames for David, such as 'Spooky Drew', and greet him with witty jibes, such as, "Hello David. How am I?" It is good-natured banter, but beyond that, we try to steer clear of David's work in social situations, and for good reason. We find that people are either so enthusiastic about the subject, that they won't talk about anything else, persistently trying to procure an impromptu reading, or they argue that it is all a load of rubbish, challenging David to prove the contrary. Neither scenario is ideal when you are out for a relaxing evening or in the queue at Asda.

We never raise the subject ourselves or force our beliefs. Those who are interested, seek David out professionally. If people choose not to believe in the spirit world, that's fine. Why argue? Everyone finds out the truth in the end.

The second group, are the friends we meet as a result of David's work; the ones who have seen him work and know his worth. These are the ones we would invite to our house-warming circles. Yes, instead of house-warming parties, we have always held a séance when we move to a new home. It may sound odd, but it creates a calm atmosphere in the house and brings high spirit close. While our 'normal' friends would probably view this as creepy, this group are more than happy to share in the experience.

Around a year or so after our wedding, my father asked me how I was enjoying married life. I answered, "I have never had so many friends."
"That's nice." He answered, looking pleased.
Then I thought for a moment and added. "Or so many enemies."

Many of the people whom David has helped, evolved into lifelong friends, but on the flip side of the coin are those who believe that what he does is the work of the devil. Without exception, these are people who don't know him personally, and they are mostly religious extremists. In their zeal, they have threatened to slash his tyres, and once he even had to have a police escort to a theatre, because born-again Christians had vowed not to let him go on stage without physical harm. They were angrily picketing outside as plainclothes police ferried David in the back way like a rock star.

It is amazing to think that Christians could behave in this way, but at least mediums are in good company.

In Matthew 12:24, Jesus is also accused of doing the devil's work.

In the 1980's, David ran a weekly Psychic Club at The Ship and Royal in Lytham St Annes, Lancashire. We stumbled across the venue after David helped the landlord with a ghostly problem. The detail on this can be found in David's autobiography, *'The Other Side; A Psychic's Story.'* I will give you the Reader's Digest version.

The licensees were being frightened half to death by all manner of eerie goings-on. It began with the usual events; glasses smashing on their own; lightbulbs blowing when they walked into a room. Then it evolved into the more bizarre. The landlady found the evening's takings arranged in a neat circle on the floor, then her chair moved – with her in it!

This final straw inspired them to seek help. Enter David in full ghost-busting mode.

He was escorted upstairs to the living quarters and the closed-off Figurehead Bar. The room was as inhospitable as its troublesome resident.

Genuine ship's figureheads lined the walls, like giants in sleep, and in one dark corner sat a translucent little old man, wearing a colourful waistcoat.

He peered at David, who, to his surprise, acknowledged him, and they began to talk. It turned out that all the trouble had been caused by this one character, who was reluctant to call time on his old haunt.

David convinced the old boy, who had been killed in a plane crash, to ease back on his antics, but once the couple realised it wasn't some demonic entity, they were much more relaxed about the situation. As David enjoyed a pint with them afterwards, he asked if he could book the disused room to hold a weekly meeting. It was the perfect size and the atmosphere was ideal. Thus, the Psychic Club was born.

Each Thursday evening there would be a psychic demonstration, either by David or a guest medium and on the first Thursday of every month, members could attend the psychic development circle. Here, like-minded people sat each month, to develop their psychic abilities and receive some spiritual teaching, often directly from those in spirit, through David, courtesy of his trance work.

The first meeting was an evening of clairvoyance, to introduce David to the new members. We arrived early, as usual, so that I could set up the room.

My first job was to place a table outside the

Figurehead Bar, at the top of the stairs. From here I could distribute brochures, take tickets and manage David's diary. The landlady had stacked around fifty chairs for us to use, and as I helped set them out, I hoped enough people would have heard about the event to make the evening worthwhile.

Twenty-five minutes before kick-off, the first few groups of people began to filter upstairs to take their seats. Within fifteen minutes there was a hum in the room, and the chairs were almost filled. I looked over the banister of the wide, sweeping staircase. It was packed with people waiting for tickets. I began the apologies, explaining to people that there were only two or three seats left, but most said they were prepared to stand, so I let them in, trying to keep track of space through the glass in the double doors. With five minutes to go, the room was packed to bursting, and I suddenly realised that perhaps I was too easily persuaded. We had to be breaching fire regulations.

The stairs were still filled with people, and I knew I would have to tactfully refuse entry to them all. They weren't happy, but I explained the situation and offered advance tickets for the following week. As I spoke to the people at the front of the queue, I heard a commotion further down the stairs.
"We were here before you! It's full anyway!"
It was David, being held back by the crowd. They thought he was trying to push in. It was hilarious, but I had to intervene, so I called down the staircase, "If you don't let him up, there won't *be* an evening of clairvoyance."

A journalist was among the people who managed to get a seat. The Gazette that week led with, 'Unforeseen Success of Psychic Club."

At these weekly meetings, we came to know some lovely people, including one gentleman who came to be one of David's dearest friends.

Igor Gridneff, (pronounced 'Eager', as he would insist – the other version being a peasant name, apparently,) was of Russian descent, though he was born in India. A stage and TV actor, he had also been a circus master and had retired to Lytham-St-Annes. He was fascinated by the spirit world, and particularly enjoyed the circles, where he could speak with Pepe about circus life and the after-life. He never missed a psychic club meeting and would meet with David every Sunday afternoon to put the world to rights over a few beers.

He taught David how to 'work the round'. That is to say, how to hold an audience's attention when you are in the midst of them. This was useful advice, as David was sometimes called upon to address a crowd in cabaret-style surroundings, and there was certainly a knack in keeping those behind engaged while passing on a message to someone out front.

I loved Igor's company and enjoyed our conversations tremendously - not that we always agreed. After the meetings, the psychic club gang would chat in the bar until closing time. We would often debate spiritual and theological matters.

I was in my mid-twenties, and he would have been almost sixty, but we were good pals.

He passed in 1990 after we had left the area and moved to Wales. It was cancer. We didn't get to say goodbye, but he still visits us from time to time, and has even spoken in circle, this time from the other side of the veil. I very much look forward to meeting up with him again one day and perhaps putting a different world to rights.

It was during this era that we met Maureen and her son, Mark. Their friendship was to become very important to us. They have both been a valuable help over the years in supporting and promoting David's work.

When we met Maureen, she was a smartly dressed businesswoman in her forties. Although short in stature, her shock of red hair and capricious demeanour, dictated she never went unnoticed in a room. A friend of hers had been to see David and reported back that he had predicted three life-changing events, of which she was highly sceptical. Within a few weeks, however, all three had come true. On hearing this, Maureen booked to see David for a reading, and also for spiritual healing. She had been diagnosed with diverticulitis, and her Harley Street specialist told her she needed a colostomy.

A few weeks after seeing David, she turned up on our doorstep one evening, with a tray of eggs (her husband had an egg farm), a bottle of champagne, and a big smile. She had been back to her specialist, and a further x-ray showed her condition to be completely healed. She was thrilled and told us that she had some promotional experience, offering her services to help publicise David's work. She was tremendously enthusiastic – a real force of nature, and at first, we weren't quite sure what had hit us!

It is the most important thing in the world, to David, that people hear what he has to say about life being eternal and how this life is so very important. It is why he is here. Whether people believe what he says is up to them. All he has to do is make sure they have the opportunity to listen, then his job is done.

In the coming months and years, true to her word, Maureen secured invitations for him to appear on TV and radio across the UK and even worldwide. He appeared on Kilroy, The Time, The Place, The James Whale Show, Esther, and Weird Wales. The theatres he was filling were getting larger, and a couple of hauntings he attended even made the TV news.

David, despite appearances, has always been a bag of nerves when appearing in public. He hid it quite well, but he always hated that side of his work. A singer or comedian can rehearse. He has to walk out cold, without a clue what – if anything- is going to happen. I remember one time at a theatre, he was in the wings, about to go on stage when I noticed the manageress approaching. Stressed to distraction, he introduced me to her, "This is my wife, Carol." Then he walked out on stage.

Now, I was faced with a choice. Should I say nothing and let her call me Carol all night, or should I humiliate him and say, "My husband just got my name wrong"?

Of course, I went with the latter. Spousal loyalty can only stretch so far, and I would be able to dine out on this for years! I still tease him about it today. Maybe I should have kept quiet and saved him the embarrassment, but in the words of Meat Loaf, 'I would do anything for love – but I won't do that.'

Truthfully, I understood how stressed he was, and even shared in his nervousness. At times it was as if I was walking out onto that stage or in front of those cameras myself. I would feel nauseous and the room would spin. If I was at home, waiting for him to appear live on TV or radio I would be pacing the floor, my head ready to burst. Once he began, I would be still. He always spoke well, and as his nerves calmed, so did mine. Once I knew he was alright, so was I.

People would say, "He is always so relaxed and confident." I would smile at how they perceived him to be, knowing it was far from the truth.

Soon he had opened healing clinics in Edinburgh, London and the North West, and had various regular radio spots across the UK. There were world tours, documentaries about his work, international magazine articles, and eventually, he wrote books, so he could reach a new audience.

It is strange how certain people at different times, found themselves drawn to David, quite out of the blue. Often they came at a time in their lives when they needed a helping hand and sometimes they stayed, hoping to repay the favour.

In circles, Maureen was often told to, "Bring the boy." She had no idea who they meant, until her youngest son, Mark, came to join the group, and Dr. Albert told him they were glad to see him - at last.

At that time, Mark was a free-spirited young man in his twenties. I think his initial incentive to learn more about the world of spirit, was the realisation that the topic could be an interesting conversation starter for the young ladies. In those days he travelled a lot, spending months in warmer climates, but when he was home he would accompany his mum to David's meetings, and his fascination for this subject grew. Before long, he was a close friend of the Drew family, helping spread the word in any way he could.

I suspect a fair amount of our acquaintances regard us, if not as crazy, at least a bit on the eccentric side. David was eventually forced to retire from his public work, due to poor health, instead focusing on his writing and occasionally helping to find missing persons, both of which can be done from his wheelchair in his own good time.

Inevitably, our lifestyle changed somewhat when this happened.

I took a couple of 'normal' jobs – a florist and a shoe shop - and, for the most part, got on well with my colleagues, but I was very aware that they thought me strange. On a Monday morning, they would chat about their weekend. "I took my mum to Snowdonia Nurseries." "We had a barbeque." "I started knitting a jumper." "What about you, Jane? Did you do something nice?"

I would smile sheepishly from behind a stack of boxes, dismayed to be required to enter into the dreaded conversation, which always culminated in me sounding like a weirdo.

"Well, it was the launch party for David's new book," or "Err, we went to Channel Four studios," or, "Actually, Ricky Tomlinson came down to have a drink with us," or even, "That Austrian documentary they made about David was aired." I would cringe every time I was cornered into one of these conversation stoppers, scolding myself for not being quick enough to think up a boring lie. I knew what they were thinking behind those bewildered eyes. What a nut-job! And who can blame them? Nine times out of ten, my answer was something bizarre. They probably thought I was delusional – even though I edited out the *really* weird stuff, like, "Oh, and I chatted to a native American Chief who's been dead four-hundred years."

Finding myself in this situation, I was reminded of Barry, a very good friend of ours who was a member of David's Psychic Development Circle.

He was in his fifties, worked for the Inland Revenue, and first came to us on the heels of a lady friend, who was the instigator of their visits, but soon fell by the wayside. Barry, however, never missed a circle. He lived in the West Midlands and worked in London, but drove to Llandudno once a month without fail, for the circle.

He would phone us in the afternoon, from his car, "I'm just leaving the House of Lords now. I've been in meetings all day. Should be there on time, but if I'm a bit late, hang on for me."

We all thought it was a tall story, but we liked Barry and took it in good part. Each month he would arrive with his leather man-bag (regarded as an eccentricity at the time), and yet another unbelievable story.

"I would have been here sooner, but I popped into Londis for a sandwich, and they were being held up at gunpoint. I grabbed hold of the guy and held on to him until the police came."

"I went to a wedding last weekend and fell into the drum-kit and ruined the first dance. The bride was furious."

"I should have flown back from the States last Monday, but I had to stay over because I was so drunk, they wouldn't let me on the plane."

We enjoyed his far-fetched stories. They were always entertaining and surprisingly detailed for fairy-tales.

It was astounding to realise we had done him an injustice. Our local Londis *had* been held up at gunpoint.

He was taken suddenly, and we didn't find out about the other stories until the day of his funeral.

We drove down to the Midlands for the service. David was uneasy, as he had been asked to speak – a recurring theme in his world. He knew he would struggle to hold it together. When it came down to it, his emotional eulogy more than did Barry justice, and everyone in the crowded room, left with a lump in their throat.

Afterwards, at the wake, mourners shared stories of Barry's antics. David was talking to a smartly dressed gentleman.
"You were Barry's boss? Who is your boss then?"
"No-one has ever asked me that," the easy-going, suited gentleman replied. "I suppose you would say it's the Chancellor of the Exchequer."
It seems Barry really did attend meetings in the Houses of Parliament.

Sharing stories that day, we realised that all of Barry's unbelievable anecdotes had been true after all.

The regular circle goers were generally a good fit; like-minded people who became more so over time. Occasionally, however, there was a square-peg.

Before every development circle, David would stress the responsibility that goes along with using psychic gifts, and that the process of developing extensively would take years. One lady sat for a few weeks, then left the circle and set herself up as a practicing psychic. David was mortified. She had ignored his advice and was out there possibly misleading people. I told him it was her ego; that it wasn't his fault, but he was sickened by it. He didn't like to think he was responsible for putting someone out there who was misleading people.

In the past, some neighbours have regarded us with apprehension and a degree of curiosity. After all, what sort of people would take on the dreaded murder house without a second thought?

One house in Llandudno, North Wales, where we lived for a while, had a room on the top floor which we used for holding circles, and also as a peaceful place to meditate. We called it the chapel because it was an ideal place to pray and reflect. The positive atmosphere there had become electric; the powerful feeling of love and the presence of high-spirit, took your breath.

A few weeks after we left that place, the new occupiers phoned us in a state of panic. They wanted to know what we had done in that room, and if David could exorcise it.

I reassured them that there was nothing bad there, and they needn't be afraid.

I was impressed that, without any knowledge that we had used that room for circles, the new residents had been able to feel the atmosphere.

When it comes to family members, they fall into various categories. Naturally, our children and immediate family completely understand and share our belief in God and communion with the spirit world. This way of life is as normal to them as it is to us.

Then there are those more distant relatives, in the outer circle, who accept our lifestyle but see it as something strange. Next are those who don't comment on it at all. Some of them have firm religious beliefs which clash with ours and could have the potential to create conflict. Others have no beliefs at all and are perhaps open-minded. I am sure some of these think we are crazy, but despite this, we get on well with all family members, usually by avoiding the subject of David's work when we are unsure how it would be received.

David's brother Tim, however, is the first to contact him when a family member is seriously ill or needs help, and his sister, Helen loves to get a message from spirit.

My mum always embraced how special David is, and loved to attend his meetings – despite the occasional mother-in-law joke.

Having a Psychic Medium for a dad, our children,

Ayesha, Sian, and John, have taken some stick over the years, but they always bore it well. There was some teasing at school, but nothing too hard-core – after all, you don't really want to upset your mate, when you're not sure if their dad could put a whammy on you!

At school, they called Ayesha 'Wednesday Adams'. Although inwardly sensitive, Ayesha always stood her corner and didn't take any prisoners. A talented artist, she never quite escaped the classroom and is a college lecturer now. I doubt her students are aware that, after sitting in psychic development circles with her dad, she is a bit of a 'spooky drew' herself, and occasionally sees people in spirit.

Sian was three years her junior and less confident. Kids would tease her, asking if her dad could give them the lottery numbers or the Grand National winner. Then there were the usual, 'Why didn't he see that coming?' jokes. The ones who were interested would grill her for information about the spirit world; questions she had never even thought of. She didn't appreciate this, and couldn't really answer. She considered it mundane. That stuff just happened, and she never really wondered why or how. It was boring enough having to play quietly when her dad was seeing people in his office, without having to talk about that kind of thing at school. She survived with the help of her wacky sense of humour and generous spirit.

One time at primary school, she was worried about a spelling test. David reassured her. "I'll ask Blue Cloud to come with you to school and help."

She got three out of ten questions right. With hindsight, David realised that perhaps he sent the wrong person.

At the next circle, Blue Cloud was indignant.
"I lived to one-hundred and twenty-four, without ever having to spell 'Wednesday'."

They were good kids, but they just couldn't help themselves when it came to practical jokes. I was furious when they swapped the sugar for salt on the guest's breakfast tables one morning; also when they plugged the baby monitor behind the bar and made strange noises to spook a particularly nervous cleaner.

Whenever David was holding one of his Psychic Weekends, the children had to occupy themselves quietly between certain hours of the day. Events were spread out across the two days; a psychic demonstration; healing; lectures and a circle.

The girls had bedrooms on the top floor of Blue Cloud Lodge, where there was a communal bathroom.

One Saturday evening after the day's events were finished, Ayesha saw her sister enter the bathroom, and decided to lay in wait and make her jump.

She knew that Sian would be a little on edge because she was shy and guests were in the house.

Eventually, Sian came out and Ayesha shouted, 'Boo!" scaring her to death.

Ayesha, still laughing, went into the bathroom herself, then quietly back to her room.

Hearing a door close, she peeped out into the hallway through the crack in the door, where she saw Sian, in her pyjamas, crouching by the bathroom, waiting to take revenge on her big sister.

At this point, Ayesha could have shown herself and made Sian aware that it must be a guest in the bathroom. Instead, delighting in the unfolding events, she watched in silence.

The guest in question was a lady in her fifties who, when she arrived, was having second thoughts about the weekend, after a taxi driver decided to tell her about the murder on the ride from the station. Her friends had persuaded her to stay, but she was very nervous.

So, the perfect storm hit! The lady exited the bathroom and Sian jumped up and shouted, "Raahh." Both of them looked equally petrified – and Ayesha was triumphant.

Sometimes, however, the joke was on them.

One morning, Sian was playing with John in the bar at Blue Cloud Lodge. She is nine years older than her little brother and was teasing him unkindly. Suddenly someone shouted, 'STOP IT'. Thinking herself found out by myself or David, she sheepishly looked all around, but there was no one there. David and I were two floors above and knew nothing of what had happened. She was reminded that day - you can't get away with much in the Drew family.

As an adult, Ayesha would come to stay at our house when we were away, to look after our cat and German Shepherd. One evening, she telephoned me.
"I can't get the dog to settle, and I keep hearing footsteps."
"Shout her into your bedroom. Let her sleep with you and she will be fine."

To be fair, hearing footsteps on the top floor of that house was common, and a handle up there was sometimes seen to be depressed as the door unlatched itself and swung open.

I heard Ayesha open the bedroom door and call the dog. "River!....River!....She won't come."
This was odd, as she was a very obedient dog. I had an idea.
"When she is out of earshot, I clap twice. It is her signal to come running. Try that."

So, Ayesha stood in her doorway and gave two claps. Immediately, River came running towards her from our bedroom.

When she was half-way across the landing, she suddenly slammed on the breaks, as two loud claps came out of our bedroom. The dog looked at Ayesha, then towards our room, not knowing which command to obey.

Someone in spirit obviously thought this was funny. Ayesha, who was alone in the three-story house, did not appreciate the humour.

John also suffered the usual teasing at school, but despite the embarrassment, remained proud of his dad. Each morning we would climb the stone steps by Chester's Eastgate clock, onto the city walls to begin the walk to school.

We would see squirrels playing on the site of the Roman barracks, and skirt the banks of the river Dee, where water lapped against the city wall. Then we would stop to look at the blue-blossom of a particular tree on the route, which we had claimed for our own.

The walk home from school at half-past three took us a different way. We would pass under the city walls, passing by the Cathedral and through the city centre.

On Werburgh Street was a small church shop. One day, John was taken with a colourful, children's illustrated Bible in the window. It had been a rough day for him. I delved into my pocket to see how much money I had. Just enough.
"You can have it if you'd like." His face lit up.

"Can I have some sweets too?" There was a sweet shop a little further down the street.

"I haven't got money for both. You will have to choose." He stood in silence, his face making a fist with concentration. I offered some help. "The sweets will feed your belly, but the Bible will feed your soul."
He thought for a few moments more, then the decision was made.
"My soul isn't hungry."

He was a sensitive child, but at fourteen he suddenly came into his own. His self-confidence blossomed and he became socially adept and headstrong. As he matured, he was amazed to discover just how many people had heard of his dad. Many had seen him for readings or on stage and were in awe of what they had experienced. Now the situation was reversed. The teasing was finally laid to rest.

John was much younger than his sisters, and David's work landscape was already changing by the time he came along.

His dad was writing, seeing people privately, and appearing in the media, but there were fewer large public demonstrations, due to David struggling to stand for long periods.

After years of begging him to go to a doctor, it was around this time that he finally agreed.

I was so relieved that his condition was going to be treated at last.

When the consultation was over, I was eager to hear the diagnosis.
"What did he say?"
"He bent down, put his fingers on my feet, and told me it was ok because he could feel a pulse. He doesn't want to see me again. I told you I was fine."

I was crest-fallen. There was obviously something very wrong.

Deep down, he knew it, which is why he finally agreed to the appointment, but now he could bury his head again and pretend it would all go away. It didn't.

At first, he was too vain to use a stick, but in time he realised he would have to bite down on his pride. In a matter of a few months, he was also struggling on the stairs. I suggested a stair-lift, and he was insulted. Old people use stair-lifts, and he was still in his fifties. At last, he saw the sense in it and arranged to have one installed.

Before long, I noticed that the only time he agreed to leave the house was if we were going in the car. He tried to conceal it, but I could see he couldn't walk more than a few steps.

A friend suggested a mobility scooter, which was a sensible idea, but David was mortified. He was not going to be seen on one of those. It was far too embarrassing. In the end, he succumbed. It took quite a while for him to accept his new wheels, but at last, he began going out in the fresh air, and his quality of life improved.

By the time David was referred to a specialist, he could hardly walk at all, Peripheral Vascular Disease had gone too far. In theory, he needed an operation to unblock his arteries, but by this time his lungs were not strong enough to withstand the procedure. Chronic Obstructive Pulmonary Disease had taken hold and he faced his future years in a wheelchair.

It was a devastating scenario to be presented with. I was heartbroken for him, but he was still my hero. We have always said we can get through anything so long as we are together.

It was a close call, but thankfully, David was able to fulfill his ambition of walking both his girls down the aisle.

The first was Sian. She married Gary in 2014 at the St Georges Hotel, Llandudno. David was worried about the length of the aisle. He was able to walk a short distance at the time, if he used a stick, but he wanted to do this without any aids. When the day came, he gathered all his strength and excelled himself. He even managed to stand-up long enough to deliver his father of the bride speech, which was both touching and hilarious - and ended up on YouTube. Not a dry eye in the house – least of all his!

Ayesha married Nathan three years later in 2017. Their wedding was held at the Quay Hotel in Deganwy. This was a trickier prospect, because by now David was in a wheelchair, and could manage very few steps. However, in the end, with a little logistical planning, it was beautifully executed. John, wearing my dad's fob watch, walked Ayesha half-way down the aisle, and David, who was waiting in a seat, exchanged places with him and walked her the rest of the way to the alter. His speech that day, was, of course, emotional. By now he was well known to be brought to tears at the drop of a hat when it came to his kids, who lightened the mood by enjoying a hearty laugh at his expense.

Our clan was growing. Time had seen us add two sons-in-law and soon three granddaughters, Sarah, Willow and Paisley, to our crazy brood.

We are all here for a reason. Opportunities relevant to our purpose are placed in our path. Most of us don't know why we are here, so we just have to do our best and pray we get something right.

David's circumstance is unusual. He *does* know why he is having this life. He is here to tell people that their loved ones live on and that there is nothing to fear in death, so long as we have lived our lives well.

Like a vicar's wife, I always expected to take second place to his work. That is how it should be. I am content, however, that when one of us passes over, there will never be more than a thin veil between us.

As the psychic's wife, I have come to realise that my role is to help David keep the message alive. I would like to think of myself, if not as the wind beneath his wings, at least perhaps the breeze upon his brow.

It is something very special to believe what you have never seen. David sees some marvelous things, and by my proximity to him, I have shared many of these experiences.

I realise that most of you will not have personally witnessed the wonders of the spirit world, but how fantastic it is when people have faith in what they haven't seen. I am envious of that.

As a girl, when my parents took me to church, I sat in the choir stalls, listening to the Rector and trying my best to understand.

I believed in God, but there were things in the teachings that I couldn't accept. I went to confirmation classes but still couldn't find the answers. I thought I was doubting God, but it was the contradictions of organized religion that confused me.

Such as;

In the story of Adam and Eve, God tells Adam that if he eats the fruit of the tree he will die the same day. Eve is told by a talking snake, to eat the fruit and they will not die. They both eat it and don't die. Was the snake right and God wrong?

In Genesis 32, Jacob wrestles with God, and God pleads with him to let Him go.

Exodus 4:24, God tries – and fails – to kill Moses.

The Bible tells us not to cut the hair on the side of our heads or summon people to prayer with bells. It instructs us not to call anyone 'father', and not to eat pork

Even the Christmas story was confusing. I couldn't find a mention of three kings or a stable anywhere. It did, however, mention some men who followed the stars and the house where Jesus was born.

Since knowing David, the blanks have been filled in and now it all makes sense. He explained how the Bible is like an overgrown garden. We have to chop away the weeds to find the flowers. There is a lot of truth in there if we ignore the man-made nonsense. Religious leaders who would have you believe every word of the Bible, are overlooking the fact that it was written by fallible men, and translated from language to language, many times.

One frequently recurring theme in church, was that Jesus suffered and died to save us. I struggled with this one. How did Jesus' murder mean I was saved? I couldn't see the connection, and it was never explained.

I can see now that Christ was with God in heaven, and made the sacrifice of coming down to earth, because mankind was lost and needed direction. He didn't die to save us, He *lived* to save us, by his teachings.

God is a loving parent. I imagine it could make Him sad if we don't believe in Him, but I suspect He believes in us, nonetheless. We love our children, even when they mess-up. It would be heartbreaking if they disowned us, but worse if they disappoint us with their bad behaviour.

It is my experience that each sibling views his father through different eyes. To one he is a storyteller and counsellor, another sees an accomplished sportsman and handyman. The first may fondly remember him as easy-going and forgiving, while the second feels the pressure of living up to his expectations. Perhaps he taught one about nature – the flora and fauna, the other, how to mend a car.

Each child sees a slightly different personality, but they are siblings, and even if their visions differ, all love their father and all are right. No matter what our religion or point of view, God is a loving parent to everyone
.

We live in sad times where society is quick to raise its voice in judgement and ashamed to speak of things that can't be seen or touched. God is the new taboo. Bad language is accepted, but to speak His name is to risk ridicule or offence.

If all you take away from these pages, is the realization that how you behave in this life is directly proportional to your wellbeing afterwards, I am content with that.

The devil wants you to eat, drink and be merry; to do anything to make yourself happy in this life, as if there are no consequences. He is the voice at your shoulder who tells you that you deserve better; to take the easy path, which is the road to him.

My life as the wife of a psychic, has certainly been unique; a fabulous roller coaster ride that I never expected.

Now I leave these pages to go and cook David's dinner, I bring my book to a close, I hope it has all the attributes of the perfect skirt; that it was long enough to cover the essentials but short enough to hold your attention.

I don't expect everyone who reads this to become a believer, and that's okay. More important than what you believe in this life, is how you behave. If you can't accept that there is anything after death, be nice anyway. Leave the world a better place than when you found it. What do you have to lose? When you wake up dead - you'll be glad you did.

Look upon that which you cannot see.
Listen to what you cannot hear.
Accept what you do not deserve
And reject all that is wrong.

David Drew.

Stairway to Heaven

DAVID DREW

Is there really a heaven and hell? Is it true we have many lives? What happens when we die? Should we believe all we read in the Bible?

David Drew is well known as a spiritual medium and healer, but he has also been called a twentieth-century prophet and even a miracle worker. He has astounded people all his life with his remarkable psychic powers and his unique spiritual knowledge.

In this book, he lays down, in a down-to-earth style, answers to questions which have puzzled people over the ages.

This book could change your entire outlook on life.

AVAILABLE FROM
AMAZON; KINDLE; AUDIBLE; ITUNES

The Other Side: A Psychic's Story

DAVID DREW

The true story of a young boy who sees ghosts.

This autobiographical work examines the life of a child who interacts with the dead on a daily basis, and how this affected his family and ultimately, his adult life.

His story begins in the smog of the West Midlands, with his mother struggling to bring up four children alone. When her son sees family members who died before he was born, including the sister he never knew he had, she takes him to a psychiatrist. When the boy gives the doctor a message from his dead wife, he is promptly discharged.

The teenage David struggles to understand why he is different and is expelled from school at fifteen.

His adult life takes us on a journey filled with poltergeists, bombs, and startling revelations.

AVAILABLE FROM
AMAZON; KINDLE; AUDIBLE; ITUNES

Further Sources

www.daviddrew.co.uk

www.spiritlightbydaviddrew.wordpress.com

Twitter:
@davidpsychic
@psychics_wife

Facebook:
David Drew. Psychic Medium
Stairway to Heaven

Instagram:
the_psychics_wife
david.drew.psychic

YouTube:
David Drew psychic